15 days
of prayer with
SAINT EUGENE DE MAZENOD

15 days
of prayer series

On a journey, it's good to have a guide. Even great saints took spiritual directors or confessors with them on their itineraries toward sanctity. Now you can be guided by the most influential spiritual figures of all time. The 15 Days of Prayer series introduces their deepest and most personal thoughts.

This popular series is perfect if you are looking for a gift, or if you want to be introduced to a particular guide and his or her spirituality. Each volume contains:

- ◌ A brief biography of the saint or spiritual leader
- ◌ A guide to creating a format for prayer or retreat
- ◌ Fifteen meditation sessions with focus points and reflection guides

15 days
of prayer with
SAINT EUGENE DE MAZENOD

BERNARD DULLIER

FOREWORD BY
RONALD ROLHEISER, O.M.I.

TRANSLATED BY
EDWARD CAROLAN, O.M.I.

NEW CITY PRESS
Hyde Park, NY

Published in the United States by New City Press
202 Cardinal Rd., Hyde Park, NY 12538
www.newcitypress.com
©2009 New City Press
(English translation)

This book is a translation of *Prier 15 Jours avec Eugene de Mazenod*,
published in 2001 by Nouvelle Cité, Montrouge, France

Cover design by Durva Correia

Library of Congress Cataloging-in-Publication Data:

Dullier, Bernard.
  [Prier 15 jours avec Eugene de Mazenod. English]
  15 days of prayer with Saint Eugene de Mazenod / Bernard Dullier ;
foreword by Ronald Rolheiser.
      p. cm.
    ISBN 978-1-56548-320-0 (pbk. : alk. paper)
  1. Mazenod, Charles-Joseph-Eugene de, Saint, 1782-1861—
Meditations. 2. Spiritual life—Catholic Church. I. Title. II. Title:
Fifteen days of prayer with Saint Eugene de Mazenod.
  BX4700.M429D8513   2009
  242'.802—dc22   2009000720

Printed in the United States of America

Contents

How to Use
This Book

*A*n old Chinese proverb, or at least what I am able to recall of what is supposed to be an old Chinese proverb, goes something like this: "Even a journey of a thousand miles begins with a single step." When you think about it, the truth of the proverb is obvious. It is impossible to begin any project, let alone a journey, without taking the first step. I think it might also be true, although I cannot recall if another Chinese proverb says it, "that the first step is often the hardest." Or, as someone else once observed, "the distance between a thought and the corresponding action needed to implement the idea takes the most energy." I don't know who shared that perception with me but I am certain it was not an old Chinese master!

With this ancient proverbial wisdom, and the not-so-ancient wisdom of an unknown contemporary sage still fresh, we move from proverbs to presumptions. How do these relate to the task before us?

I am presuming that if you are reading this introduction it is because you are contemplating a journey. My presumption is that you are preparing for a spiritual journey and that you have taken at least some of the first steps necessary to prepare for this journey. I also presume, and please excuse me if I am making too many presumptions, that in your preparation for the spiritual journey you have determined that you need a guide. From deep within the recesses of your deepest self, there was something that called you to consider Eugene de Mazenod as a potential companion. If my presumptions are correct, may I congratulate you on this decision? I think you have made a wise choice, a choice that can be confirmed by yet another source of wisdom, the wisdom that comes from practical experience.

Even an informal poll of experienced travelers will reveal a common opinion: it is very difficult to travel alone. Some might observe that it is even foolish. Still others may be even stronger in their opinion and go so far as to insist that it is necessary to have a guide, especially when you are traveling into uncharted waters and into territory that you have not yet experienced. I am of the personal opinion that a traveling companion is welcome under all circumstances. The thought of traveling alone, to some exciting destination without someone to share the journey with does not capture my imagination or channel my enthusiasm. However, with that being noted, what is simply a matter of preference on the normal journey becomes a matter of necessity when a person embarks on a spiritual journey.

The spiritual journey, which can be the most challenging of all journeys, is experienced best with a guide, a companion, or at the very least, a friend in whom you have placed your trust. This observation is not a preference or an opinion but rather an established spiritual necessity. All of the great saints with whom I am familiar had a spiritual director or a confessor who journeyed with them. Admittedly, at times the saints might well have traveled far beyond the experience of their guide and companion but more often than not they would return to their director and reflect on their experience. Understood in this sense, the director and companion provided a valuable contribution and necessary resource. When I was learning how to pray (a necessity for anyone who desires to be a full-time and public "religious person"), the community of men that I belong to gave me a great gift. Between my second and third year in college, I was given a one-year sabbatical, with all expenses paid and all of my personal needs met. This period of time was called novitiate. I was officially designated as a novice, a beginner in the spiritual journey, and I was assigned a "master," a person who was willing to lead me. In addition to the master, I was provided with every imaginable book and any other resource that I could possibly need. Even with all that I was provided, I did not learn how to pray because of the books and the unlimited resources, rather it was the master, the companion who was the key to the experience.

One day, after about three months of reading, of quiet and solitude, and of practicing all of the methods and descriptions of prayer that were available to me, the master called. "Put away the books, forget the method, and just listen." We went into a room, became quiet, and tried to recall the presence of God, and then, the master simply prayed out loud and permitted me to listen to his prayer. As he prayed, he revealed his hopes, his dreams, his struggles, his successes, and most of all, his relationship with God. I discovered as I listened that his prayer was deeply intimate but most of all it was self-revealing. As I learned about him, I was led through his life experience to the place where God dwells. At that moment I was able to understand a little bit about what I was supposed to do if I really wanted to pray.

The dynamic of what happened when the master called, invited me to listen, and then revealed his innermost self to me as he communicated with God in prayer, was important. It wasn't so much that the master was trying to reveal to me what needed to be said; he was not inviting me to pray with the same words that he used, but rather that he was trying to bring me to that place within myself where prayer becomes possible. That place, a place of intimacy and of self-awareness, was a necessary stop on the journey and it was a place that I needed to be led to. I could not have easily discovered it on my own.

The purpose of the volume that you hold in your hand is to lead you, over a period of fifteen days or, maybe more realistically, fifteen prayer periods, to a place where prayer is possible. If you already have a regular experience and practice of prayer, perhaps this volume can help lead you to a deeper place, a more intimate relationship with the Lord.

It is important to note that the purpose of this book is not to lead you to a better relationship with Eugene de Mazenod, your spiritual companion. Although your companion will invite you to share some of his deepest and most intimate thoughts, your companion is doing so only to bring you to that place where God dwells. After all, the true measurement of all companions for the journey is that they bring you to the place where you need to be, and then they step back, out of the picture. A guide who brings you to the desired destination and then sticks around is a very unwelcome guest!

Many times I have found myself attracted to a particular idea or method for accomplishing a task, only to discover that what seemed to be inviting and helpful possessed too many details. All of my energy went to the mastery of the details and I soon lost my enthusiasm. In each instance, the book that seemed so promising ended up on my bookshelf, gathering dust. I can assure you, it is not our intention that this book end up in your bookcase, filled with promise, but unable to deliver.

There are three simple rules that need to be followed in order to use this book with a measure of satisfaction.

Place: It is important that you choose a place for reading that provides the necessary atmosphere for reflection and that does not allow for too many distractions. Whatever place you choose needs to be comfortable, have the necessary lighting, and, finally, have a sense of "welcoming" about it. You need to be able to look forward to the experience of the journey. Don't travel steerage if you know you will be more comfortable in first class and if the choice is realistic for you. On the other hand, if first class is a distraction and you feel more comfortable and more yourself in steerage, then it is in steerage that you belong.

My favorite place is an overstuffed and comfortable chair in my bedroom. There is a light over my shoulder, and the chair reclines if I feel a need to recline. Once in a while, I get lucky and the sun comes through my window and bathes the entire room in light. I have other options and other places that are available to me but this is the place that I prefer.

Time: Choose a time during the day when you are most alert and when you are most receptive to reflection, meditation, and prayer. The time that you choose is an essential component. If you are a morning person, for example, you should choose a time that is in the morning. If you are more alert in the afternoon, choose an afternoon time slot; and if evening is your preference, then by all means choose the evening. Try to avoid "peak" periods in your daily routine when you know that you might be disturbed. The time that you choose needs to be your time and needs to work for you.

It is also important that you choose how much time you will spend with your companion each day. For some it will be possible to set aside enough time in order to read and reflect on all the material that is offered for a given day. For others, it might not be possible to devote one time to the suggested material for the day, so the prayer period may need to be extended for two, three, or even more sessions. It is not important how long it takes you; it is only important that it works for you and that you remain committed to that which is possible.

For myself I have found that fifteen minutes in the early morning, while I am still in my robe and pajamas and before my morning coffee, and even before I prepare myself for the day, is the best time. No one expects to see me or to interact with me because I have not yet "announced" the fact that I am awake or even on the move. However, once someone hears me in the bathroom, then my window of opportunity is gone. It is therefore important to me that I use the time that I have identified when it is available to me.

Freedom: It may seem strange to suggest that freedom is the third necessary ingredient, but I have discovered that it is most important. By freedom I understand a certain "stance toward life," a "permission to be myself and to be gentle and understanding of who I am." I am constantly amazed at how the human person so easily sets himself or herself up for disappointment and perceived failure. We so easily make judgments about ourselves and our actions and our choices, and very often those judgments are negative, and not at all helpful.

For instance, what does it really matter if I have chosen a place and a time, and I have missed both the place and the time for three days in a row? What does it matter if I have chosen, in that twilight time before I am completely awake and still a little sleepy, to roll over and to sleep for fifteen minutes more? Does it mean that I am not serious about the journey, that I really don't want to pray, that I am just fooling myself when I say that my prayer time is important to me? Perhaps, but I prefer to believe that it simply means that I am tired and I just wanted a little more sleep. It doesn't mean anything more than that. However, if I make it mean more than that, then I can become discouraged, frustrated, and put myself into a state where I might more easily give up. "What's the use? I might as well forget all about it."

The same sense of freedom applies to the reading and the praying of this text. If I do not find the introduction to each day helpful, I don't need to read it. If I find the questions for reflection at the end of the appointed day repetitive, then I should choose to close the book and go my own way. Even if I discover that the reflection offered for the day is not the one that I prefer and that the one for the next day seems more inviting, then by all means, go on to the one for the next day.

That's it! If you apply these simple rules to your journey you should receive the maximum benefit and you will soon find yourself at your destination. But be prepared to be surprised. If you have never been on a spiritual journey you should know that the "travel brochures" and the other descriptions that you might have heard are nothing compared to the real thing. There is so much more than you can imagine.

A final prayer of blessing suggests itself:
Lord, catch me off guard today. Surprise me with some moment of
        beauty or pain
So that at least for the moment
I may be startled into seeing that you
    are here in all your splendor,
Always and everywhere,
Barely hidden,
Beneath,
Beyond,
Within this life I breathe.

Frederick Buechner

Rev. Thomas M. Santa, CSsR
Liguori, Missouri

A Brief Chronology

A Saint for Dysfunctional Families

Saints tend to have a certain folklore surrounding their lives. Their virtues are lauded and put into the spotlight, giving the impression that they were less like the rest of us, with our flaws and weaknesses.

The reading of Eugene de Mazenod's correspondence would lead one to conclude that he was not a plaster saint! His was not the perfect family or problem-free life. Eugene's family divorced, he struggled with his ego and anger, and suffered through stressful personal situations. Each experience shaped him into a man that people remembered as inspiring dignity, building community, and changing lives by responding to the needs of those most abandoned.

1781:

> Charles Joseph Eugene de Mazenod was born to parents who had an arranged marriage. His father, Charles-Antoine de Mazenod, a highly educated and

17

high ranking official, was President of the Court of Accounts. He lived wildly beyond his means, and married a wealthy, but middle-class, younger woman: Marie-Rose Joannis. They had three children: Charlotte-Elizabeth, who died at age five, Charles-Joseph Eugene, the only boy, and Charlotte-Eugenie Antoinette, born three years after Eugene. The family lived a happy and privileged life, surrounded by a dozen servants.

1788–1795:

The French Revolution forced the de Mazenods to flee France, first traveling to Turin, Italy, then pooling their money with other refugees to charter a boat to Venice.

In Venice, unable to afford to send Eugene to school, a neighbor, Fr. Bartolo Zinelli, tutored him at no charge.

The stress of exile, differences in their education, opposite ideas about money, meddling in-laws and a 15-year age difference contributed to the divorce of his parents. Marie-Rose and Eugene's sister returned to France in 1795.

1796–1802:

From Venice, Eugene, his father and uncle traveled to Naples, in an effort to stay ahead of the French armies and bad business deals. In 1799, they arrived in Palermo, Italy, where due to the friendship of the Duke and Duchess of Cannizzaro, Eugene lived a life of luxury. The Duchess put Eugene in charge of distributing her money to the poor. She was a good influence on his life. At her death in 1802, he mourned her as a "second mother." Shortly after, his own mother had him return to France.

1803–1806:

In France, Eugene began searching for a direction for his life. He considered marriage, but only as a business deal. His mother found two possible marriage partners: one succumbed to tuberculosis, and the dowry of the other woman was too small. Amid all the shallowness, he had an urge to live a deeper Christian life. He joined an association at the service of prisoners and organized collections to aid the poor.

1807–1815:

Eugene had a profound experience of God's love for him during a Good Friday service. After a period of discernment, he entered the seminary of San-Sulpice in Paris. In 1811, he was ordained a priest and began to minister to those on the fringes of society. In Lent of 1813, he had services at an early hour so that the poor could attend. Unlike the clergy of that time, who preached "fire and brimstone," Eugene told them how cherished they were in God's eyes. Exhausted by overwork, he invited other priests to join him in helping to rebuild the Church that had been devastated by corruption and politics.

1816–1825:

Fr. Eugene de Mazenod and a handful of priests began preaching missions in the countryside of Provence, France.

In 1820, having returned from exile, practically penniless, Charles Antoine died at the age of 75, cared for by his brother and Eugene.

As more priests join the small group, Eugene saw the need to get formal approval from Rome and to expand beyond France. This approval would keep bishops from taking back the priest they had "loaned" to Fr. de Mazenod's work.

1826–1836:

Pope Leo XII formally approved the Constitutions and Rules of the Missionary Oblates of the most Holy and Immaculate Virgin Mary because of its witness as missionaries to the poor.

Fr. de Mazenod and Fr. Tempier went to serve as Vicars-General to the Bishop of Marseille, Canon Fortune' de Mazenod, Eugene's uncle. However, their absence left a leadership vacuum resulting in dissension in the Congregation. From 1826 to 1831, 21 men remained; 24 left.

In 1832, Fr. de Mazenod was called to Rome and ordained Bishop of Icosia in *partibus infidelium* (Icosia was a defunct Church See in Algeria). The French government, angered because the Pope had not consulted with them, stripped de Mazenod of his French citizenship and twice he found himself in disfavor with the pope.

Amid this controversy, Bishop de Mazenod worked tirelessly to give comfort to the sick and dying during the cholera epidemic of 1835.

1837–1853:

59-year-old Bishop de Mazenod takes over the Diocese of Marseille on Christmas Eve of 1837. His residence was open daily from 10 a.m. to 2 p.m. to welcome the poor or wealthy, all were treated with the same dignity and affection. He encouraged the laity to believe in their own dignity and to help reach out to the needy in their neighborhoods.

In 1840, during Ireland's famine and plague, he asked the people of his diocese to help. Wherever there was a need, he responded with spiritual or financial support, or personnel.

From 1841–1851:

Bishops throughout the world ask for Oblates for their diocese and so he sends them to Canada, England, Oregon, Sri Lanka, Texas, New York.

1854–1861:

When Pope Pius IX defined the dogma of the Immaculate Conception, Bishop de Mazenod was present in Rome.

Eugene continues to send Oblates throughout the world — Ireland, Mexico....

On May 21, 1861, Bishop de Mazenod dies at the age of 78, with Oblates praying the Salve Regina by his bedside. Of the 414 Oblates living in 1861, about 100 worked in the United States.

1975:

Beatification on October 19 by Pope Paul VI.

1995:

Canonization on December 3 by Pope John Paul II.

Foreword

*E*ugene de Mazenod, the founder of the Missionary Oblates of Mary Immaculate and former Bishop of Marseille, is not very widely known, despite being canonized as saint in 1995. More unfortunate still is the fact that his rich spirituality, which takes Christ's preferential option for the poor as its centerpiece, suffers that same anonymity. This is not surprising. Despite being a member of the religious order that he founded, I too was late in appreciating his depth and richness.

When, at the tender age of 17, I joined the Missionary Oblates of Mary Immaculate, I knew nothing really about him. I had known some good Oblate missionaries, fine men, including my older brother who was already a priest in the order, but I didn't even know the name of the man who had founded the order I had just joined. Moreover, during my novitiate year, when I was first introduced to the life and writings of Eugene, I felt more of an aversion than an affinity to him. He was, I decided then, someone who wouldn't like me, someone whose fiery temperament would send me running for cover, and someone whom I wouldn't be very comfortable with sitting at table. I liked the Oblates, I liked the mission he'd left us, but I didn't like him. His single-mindedness frightened me more than it drew me.

It took his canonization and some deeper reflection to change that. When John Paul II announced in 1995 that the church would be canonizing Eugene de Mazenod, I felt a swell of pride along with the rest of the Oblate world that our founder was to be named a saint for the universal church and for the whole world. That was special for me. Even if I didn't particularly like the man, there was a righteous pride in him being canonized. More importantly though, his canonization triggered a too long-dead curiosity inside of me: Who really was this man who founded our religious order? In ignoring him and his writings, had I missed some important boat?

I began to read again the biographies written on him, picked up his letters now published in English, and I began for the first time to see his fiery personality in a different light and to see how biblical and special his vision really was. I did a hundred and eighty-degree turn, was besotted, taken in, filled with pride, a convert, left marveling at his depth and at my own ignorance in having ignored him for so long. The capstone in this conversion came during the five days leading up to his canonization. I was in Rome, along with 800 other Oblates for the celebration. I didn't want to make this a tourist trip but a genuine pilgrimage and so instead of joining my brothers in touring churches and other sites in Rome each day, I went instead to St. Peter's and sat for hours in the Blessed Sacrament Chapel inside the Basilica and read the writings of Eugene de Mazenod. The old aversion to his fiery personality disappeared. I began to see his fiery temperament, that could so frighten the unsuspecting, for what it really was, a lover's frustration unashamed to express itself. Only a real lover rages in this way. On the day before his canonization by John Paul II, a huge banner bearing his picture draped the façade of the Basilica, announcing a new saint to the world, one whose charism I had long ago committed myself to but whose wisdom and depth I had only just discovered. I was a proud son at last!

Who is Eugene de Mazenod? What makes his spirituality so special?

15 Days of Prayer with Saint Eugene de Mazenod is designed, in essence, to do for its reader what my own journey into the person and writings of Eugene de Mazenod did for me, namely, immerse you into the person and the spirituality of an extraordinary man, a saint, whose love for Christ, for the Cross, for the Church, and especially for the poor, can serve as a model for how

someone can commit oneself more deeply to
discipleship and to Christ's preferential option
for the poor.

In this book, Bernard Dullier selects for us
the major transformative moments from the
life of Eugene de Mazenod and key texts from
his writings to invite us into a deeper vision of
discipleship and service. And he is a master:
Bernard Dullier is one of the deepest, most
respected minds in our congregation, there is
a deserved aura always when he speaks, and he
blends his sharp intellect with a deep love for
his fellow-countryman, Eugene de Mazenod,
with whom he shares the same fiery temperament, along with an equally fiery passion for
ministering to the poor. Only a fellow-countryman could so capture the soul of Eugene de
Mazenod. As a fellow-missionary under the
charism of Eugene de Mazenod, I am deeply
grateful for this book. It wonderfully honors
our founder and, more importantly, is an exceptional selection of biographical notes and auto-
biographical texts that capture the very essence
of the rich charism that was left to the Oblates
and to the world through the person and writings of St. Eugene de Mazenod.

> Ronald Rolheiser, O.M.I.
> San Antonio, Texas

The Life of Eugene de Mazenod

C harles Joseph Eugene de Mazenod was born
in Aix-en-Provence on August 1, 1782. His
father held the important position of president
of the Court of Accounts in the Parliament of
Provence and, together with his parents and
his sister, he lived his childhood years in one of
the prestigious residences (hôtels) on the Cours
Mirabeau. His family life was not as happy as it
might have been. His parents' marriage had been
one of convenience: an impoverished aristocrat
and a well-to-do bourgeois young lady aspiring
to belong to the nobility. The inevitable break-up
and divorce was to come about in 1802.

Uprooted by the whirlwind of the French
Revolution, Eugene and his family went into
exile, first to Nice and then to Venice, Naples
and finally to Palermo. His migrations were to
leave their mark on the youth and subject him
to a variety of influences, some good and some
not so good. In Venice, he was to meet a remark-
able priest in the person of Fr. Bartolo Zinelli,

whose wise counsel was to be of great help to him. In Palermo, however, he became immersed in a carefree world. He became prominent in the salons and at Court. He took unto himself the title of "Count" and forgot the piety of his boyhood.

On being recalled to France by his mother in 1802, he proceeded to enjoy life and frequented the entertainment available in the upper class residences of Aix. He was anxious to marry a rich young lady who would restore his fortune and he behaved like the rest of the young nobles who had returned from exile and who learned nothing from the Revolution and had forgotten nothing of their age-old privileged status. He continued to go to church because "a noble must practice his religion and give good example." He believed in "an all-powerful God who is a guarantee of social order." However, this light-hearted life style concentrated on pleasure made him feel a great emptiness and uselessness of his existence.

On the occasion of the Good Friday ceremonies in 1807, he was overwhelmed by the experience of seeing the figure of Christ on the Cross and he discovered the God of Love. The "conversion" caused him to decide to devote his life to Christ. In spite of the opposition from his family, he entered the seminary of San-Sulpice in 1808 and was ordained a priest in Amiens on December 21, 1811.

On his return to Aix in October 1812, he decided not to undertake any parish ministry so as to be free to exercise his priesthood where the need was greatest. He began by bringing together the abandoned youth of the city and forming his Youth Association. He also devoted his attention to prisoners and to those condemned to death. As time went on, he undertook to minister to the most neglected social classes who spoke only the Provençal language.

Eugene de Mazenod was soon to become aware that his individual efforts were not adequate to meet the needs of the apostolate he had undertaken. Therefore he brought together some priests and on January 25, 1816, they took up residence in what had been the Carmelite convent in Aix prior to the Revolution. The group took the name of "Missionaries of Provence" and they set out to evangelize the inhabitants of the more remote countryside.

There were many success stories, but there was opposition from many of the parish clergy and from some of the bishops. The work was threatened with extinction and, in order to save it, Eugene de Mazenod who had become Vicar General of Marseille in 1823, appealed to the Pope. On February 17, 1826, Pope Leo XII gave formal recognition to the new religious family under the title of the Missionary Oblates of Mary Immaculate.

The revolution of 1830, and the accession to the throne of Louis Philippe I, brought tension between the French throne and the papacy. The Pope, in an effort to declare the independence of the Church, appointed Eugene de Mazenod bishop "*in partibus*" without consulting the king. The reaction of the latter was a violent one. A press campaign was unleashed against the new bishop and he was deprived of his French citizenship. He wished to defend himself but the Pope forbade him to do so. "Deserted" by the Church, Eugene experienced a time of trial and abandonment.

A settlement would only come about in 1837, and it was then that he was appointed Bishop of Marseille. From that time onwards he fulfilled his two-fold responsibility as Superior General of a religious Congregation and pastor of the second largest city in France.

As bishop he re-organized a diocese which was in full-blown expansion. He created about 20 new parishes, renewed places of pilgrimage such as Notre Dame de la Garde, set up schools and works of charity and introduced about 30 religious congregations to the diocese. His constant concern was to attend to the needs of the most forgotten and abandoned. There was no situation of distress which left him indifferent. He visited the most repugnant areas. He was always ready to receive anyone who wished to visit him, whether the prefect of police or the fishwives, the mayor of the city or the prostitutes. He remained at his post throughout the plague epidemics, making up for the deficiencies of the civil authorities, organizing charitable works, because *"when new needs arise we must, if necessary, invent new means to meet them."*

As Superior General he was attentive to the needs of the Church wherever they occurred. He accepted the direction of numerous seminaries and took charge of Marian shrines. His special concern was to go to places where the Gospel had not yet been proclaimed, both in France and beyond its borders and so he opened his Congregation to a world dimension. In 1841, he sent six Oblates to Canada. From then onwards Oblate foundations multiplied: England, Ireland, Sri Lanka, North America, Southern Africa.

He kept up an abundant correspondence with his missionaries and it is in these letters that we find reflected the feelings of a father's heart. He shared in all their joys and in all their sorrows.

His was a fiery Mediterranean temperament and his angry outbursts could be a reflection of the Mistral, the fiercely cold wind which periodically blows down the Rhone valley. But everyone who knew him also knew that he had an impassioned love of Jesus Christ and of human beings and that he had a heart large enough to embrace the world.

He continued to exercise his twofold responsibility until his death on May 21, 1861. By that time his religious family had increased from six to 411 members and the population of his diocese from 120,000 to 340,000. On his deathbed he recommended to those around him that they *exercise charity among themselves and zeal in the outside world.*

"*Pauperes evangelizantur*" — " the Good News is being proclaimed to the poor" — These are the words from the Gospel which struck him so forcibly on a certain Good Friday and which he chose both as the motto of his religious family and the inscription on his episcopal coat of arms.

In imitation of Christ the Savior he had a passionate love for humanity. A few hours before his death he confided to one of his relatives that "*It is essential for all of you to know that God has given me a heart with an immense capacity and that he has permitted me to love immensely with it.... When I am no longer with you there will be somebody to replace my authority and who will appreciate you for your merits. But you will never have anyone who will love you as I have loved you.*"

Pope Paul VI declared Eugene Blessed on October 19, 1975, and Pope John Paul II canonized him on December 3, 1995.

Introduction

"My God, seeing the difficulties to be met in the accomplishment of one's duty, there is every reason to be discouraged and turn back. Nevertheless, the only way to go is forward. It is necessary to do so for the glory of God. Let us be courageous and trust in his grace. But in order to do so, I must, first of all, strive to become a saint."

These words were written in 1837. They outline the spiritual journey of Eugene de Mazenod and they will be our guidelines along the path we have chosen to follow in his footsteps during these fifteen days.

When the young "Count" de Mazenod entered the seminary, his spiritual director asked him to review his life and begin anew. To answer God's call, he must begin by discovering the extent of his infidelities and his sinfulness (Day 1, *Discovering One's Self*). At the same time, however, he would discover the Cross of Christ, the sign of God's love (Day 2, *Discovering the Cross of Christ*) and this would reveal to him God's unimaginable friendship (Day 3, *Discovering Christ's Friendship*).

Later, when Father de Mazenod decided
to found the Missionaries of Provence for the
evangelization of the poor, he was to realize
how much his choice of Christ had transformed
him. The worldly and self-centered young man
was being led to make choices. Having fallen in
love with God, he chose to devote his life to the
glory of this God who is love (Day 4, *Working
for the Glory of God*). It is not possible to love a
God who loves humanity without at the same
time choosing humanity and especially the most
abandoned (Day 5, *Option for Humanity*). God
brings all human beings together in one family, the Church, so that the choice of humanity
means choosing to serve the Church (Day 6, *At
the Service of the Church*).

When de Mazenod the Founder called upon
the Pope to save his work from extinction, he
had calculated all the risks to be taken. He had
accepted to be chosen by God and that is where
the risk of sainthood lies (Day 7, *Daring to Strive
for Holiness*). Of course that love of God and
human beings had to be lived out day by day
and that risked becoming routine (Day 8, *Daring
to Break Away from Routine*). In the long run he
would have to accept being disturbed, allowing
himself to be surprised by happenings and this
put his love for others at risk (Day 9, *Daring to
Love Others*).

When the newly-appointed Bishop de
Mazenod took possession of the diocese of

Marseille, he would have to take account of the extent to which his fidelity to, and his friendship with, Christ constituted a tough battle. There were frequent storms to overshadow his undertakings (Day 10, *Faithful When the Storm Strikes*). The silence of God, who sometimes seemed to be voiceless or even absent, would put his fidelity to the test (Day 11, *Faithful During Times of Darkness*). Now indeed, he was to know what it was to doubt, to be doubtful of himself and his own strength, to be doubtful of the usefulness of what he had accomplished, to be doubtful about human beings (Day 12, *Faithful in Everyday Matters*).

When the time came for the old man de Mazenod to draw up his Last Will and Testament, he would take account of the whole journey he had travelled. All the risks that he had dared to take were taken because of the Christ whom he had celebrated, received and adored in the Eucharist (Day 13, *Strengthened by the Eucharist*). Besides, he was fortunate to have sons to love, the Oblates of Mary Immaculate, whose joys and sufferings he had shared (Day 14, *Companions on the Journey*). Finally, he had always experienced an immense tenderness towards Mary, his Immaculate Mother (Day 15, *Journeying with Mary*).

At the end of these fifteen days, we shall be able to make our own the words which Saint Eugene de Mazenod addressed with such enthusiasm to those poor Provençal people, on Ash Wednesday 1813 in the Church of the Madeleine in Aix-en-Provence: *"Only God is worthy of your soul. Only God can satisfy your heart."*

For an English translation of Saint Eugene's letters, see: www.omiworld.org. Click on "Files for Animation," then click "Eugene de Mazenod."

1
Discovering
One's Self

Life presents an abundance of opportunities, often challenging, to discover one's self. Growing in self-awareness is an on-going process of evaluating one's attitudes, values, and relationships with others and God. Accepting that each of us is a flawed human, yet loved unconditionally by a merciful God, allows a person to trust in a future of possibilities.

"Jesus, my Good Master, look with compassion on your poor servant. I think that I love you but I am afraid of being mistaken. If you question me as you questioned Peter, I think I would answer as he did: 'Yes, Lord, I love you.' It would not, however, be necessary for you to put that question a third time to make me feel uneasy about the sincerity of that love.

Let me repeat, I am afraid of being mistaken, because while I believe that I love you, you can see that I do not love you at all.

"I am a sinner, I know that. I think of what I am in the eyes of God. I admire his goodness, the patience with which he has awaited me. My excess of ingratitude leaves me in a state of confusion which it is difficult to explain" (Retreat Notes, December 1–21, 1811).

/////////////

*E*ugene de Mazenod was aged thirty when he wrote these lines. In a few days he was to be ordained priest and in preparation for that event he had undertaken to make a retreat with a very specific purpose in mind:

"Purify my soul and empty my heart entirely so that the Holy Spirit will no longer find in me any obstacle to his divine workings. Fill everything in me with a love of Jesus Christ my Savior.

"Then I shall be able to live and breathe him alone, to be consumed in his love, serving him and making known how loving he is, and that men and women are foolish to look elsewhere for peace of mind which they can find in him alone" (Retreat Notes, December 1–21, 1811).

The path he had followed to reach that point had not been a smooth one. The pampered son of upper Provençal nobility and with hopes of an easygoing life lived in luxury, he had known the French Revolution of 1789 and had gone into exile. He had known the break-up of his family and the divorce of his parents for sordid reasons of financial expediency. Soon he was to become a lonely and penniless young man in Naples and later, the wheels of fortune would turn again to make him the dandy of the Court in Palermo.

His boundless energy ensured that all the human passions were his in abundance and he tasted life to the full. He liked to be surrounded by men and women friends, especially the rich and titled ones. He took pleasure in being and appearing handsome and he even adopted the title of Count to which he had no right whatever.

On returning to France in 1802, he soon took to the lifestyle of his family status and frequented the ballrooms of his native Aix-en-Provence where he went from one dance to the next and from one feast to the next.

Since his family fortunes had been partly ruined by the Revolution and he was now living well above his means, he dreamed of marrying into riches and refused an offer which he judged beneath his expectations.

"Judge for yourself what this would have meant for me: 40,000 Francs instead of the 150,000 which I expected to find!" (Letter, January 18, 1803).

"I think I shall never marry because the dowries in this country are not sufficiently large. I cannot and should not be so foolish as to marry a woman who cannot put my affairs in order" (Letter, February 12, 1803).

He did not suffer from false modesty and felt sufficiently at ease in society to want to be always at the center of events.

"*I like to be loved and especially by those whose friendship flatters my self-esteem*" (October 1808, Eugene's self-portrait for Mr. Duclaux).

He did not hesitate to use others for his own ends:

"*I have meditated on the use I make of creatures. I have no hesitation in seeing that I have been abusive in this respect, at least up to the time of my conversion. Far from using them for the purpose for which they were intended, I have made them serve my own ends, I have been concerned only with using them and taking pleasure in them*" (Retreat Notes, December 1–21, 1811).

This self-seeking was also to distance him from God even to the point of excluding him from his life and his thoughts. The God of his childhood became a stranger. His search for pleasure and social advancement left no place for the God of Jesus Christ! Of course he did not turn his back completely on his Baptism. He continued to practice and to follow the outer signs of belonging to the Church. However, God was now no more than a vague concept, a series of truths to which he adhered because of his moral and social principles:

"*I was content to use God, so to speak, to have him serve my ends, to glance in his direction in passing*" (Retreat Notes, December 1–21, 1811).

That was the path he followed. Evidently it is painful for any human being to look back on such a past and discover that he or she has been guided by a concern for appearances and the desire for immediate pleasure. It was even more difficult when that person was the proud young "Count" de Mazenod whose character did not tend towards modesty. What he discovered was all the more overwhelming for one such as he:

"God accepted me as I was. He affected not to see the damnable injuries that I continually inflicted on him; unchanging, he opened to me his loving heart" (Retreat Notes, December 1–21, 1811).

There is no point in building one's hopes on illusions, because sooner or later they will crumble to pieces leaving nothing but the distinct impression of having bypassed the essential. When it came to making a definitive commitment to building his life on God and with God, in spite of the burden of his past, Eugene discovered that it was possible to do so on one condition only: he must be open with God and drop the masks of all the personages whose roles he had tried to play in his own eyes and in those of others:

"O my God, how imperfect indeed is my conversion as yet! The roots of sin are still within me, worldly thoughts and memories still occupy my mind, the things I have renounced still strike my imagination and make unbecoming images there" (Retreat Notes, December 1–21, 1811).

Becoming aware of the truth with regard to his past life, he was ready to plunge into the future, having a clear idea of his weaknesses and a renewed confidence in God's mercy:

"*God sees to it that we can profit by the very falls into which our weak human nature can lead us.... We can redouble our trust in God, our one truly solid support.... In this way we can perfect ourselves by our very falls, so great is the mercy of God towards his poor children*" (Spiritual Conference, June 30, 1811).

A Meditation in the Company of St. Eugene

St. Eugene,

how difficult the "operation truth" must have been for you! You had to accept your mistakes, your falls, your turning back. You had to submit to being seen as you truly are.

"*Lord, what would become of me if I had not dared approach your adorable heart to consume in the midst of the fire of your love all that separates me from you?*" (Retreat Resolutions, October 12, 1808).

At last, on that December evening in 1811, you bravely dropped, one by one, all those personages whose masks you had assumed. That was what God was waiting for in order to raise you up and make you a new and upright man. Discovering yourself as you really were, you found the courage to say: "*Should I be discouraged because of all that? Certainly not, because if something has not*

been done in the past, it can be done in the future.
That is the least I expect from the infinite goodness
of my God" (Retreat Notes, December 1–21, 1811).

I too find this "operation truth" very difficult.
I feel so afraid when I come face to face with
the reality of my life, when I discover that I am
poor and naked.

However, I realize that it is indispensable for
me to know this truth. I know very well that true
love cannot grow in the midst of falsehood.

Well then, it is only on condition that I am
truthful as you were that I can experience the
overwhelming presence of God who loves me
just as I am, and who does so gratuitously and
passionately. He loves me simply because I am
precious in his eyes.

St. Eugene, obtain for me the courage to let
myself be seen by God. Take me by the hand.
Lead me to follow you in your foolish discovery of God's passionate love for me. God who
says to every man and woman:

> "You have ravished my heart,
> my sister, my bride,
> you have made me mad with love"
> (Song of Songs 4:9).

Reflection Questions

What experiences from my past are difficult to accept? What has allowed me to look at these situations, in order to better understand myself? What is my image of God, or what I call a Higher Power? God accepts and loves me "as I am"; can I accept God's unconditional love? In what way does my spiritual life influence my decisions?

2

Discovering the Cross of Christ

Focus Point

////////////

When the cross is mentioned, the first thought may be a negative one: pain, or absence of something or someone. At the heart of the cross, is the positive: a fullness of love so profound that no evil can overcome it. To know that I am loved despite my faults is humbling; it also encourages me to see God in a new light.

////////////

"The contract of union between the children of human beings and Jesus Christ was made by the Cross and on the Cross. It was on the Cross that we became attached to him, and became sharers in his merits, as though we had died with him" (Lenten Pastoral, 1860).

////////////

*E*ugene de Mazenod became aware that he was wasting his life. He had not succeeded in founding a family. He had failed to re-establish his family fortune. He no longer knew what to do with his time. He did not see any future in store for him.

"I can find nothing to entertain me. I have a strong dose of disgust for this country" (Letter to his father, March 9, 1804).

It was in the midst of this disappointment and disgust that God awaited him. It happened on Good Friday 1807, during the liturgy of the Passion, when the Cross was being solemnly presented for the veneration of the faithful. He had never before taken the time to look upon the Cross with the eyes of faith. It had never occurred to him that this Cross concerned him personally. He who was nailed to that Cross was stretching out his arms to receive him, Eugene, personally.

For the first time in his life, Eugene stopped before this man who was dying for humanity, for each man and woman individually and therefore for him. This was an overwhelming discovery of a God who was simply saying to him: "Look at me on the Cross. If I am here, it is because of you; it is because I love you."

"How can I forget the bitter tears that the sight of the Cross brought streaming from my eyes one Good Friday? Indeed they welled up from my heart. There was no stopping them.... I was in a state of mortal sin and it was precisely this which made me grieve.

But my soul was never so satisfied and never had I experienced such happiness. Despite my grief, or rather through my grief, my soul took wings towards its last end, God, its only good. The very memory of that event fills my heart with sweet satisfaction" (Retreat, December 1814).

In the depths of despair, he experienced a hand outstretched towards him. God became a Person, someone who had loved him first of all, and loved him as he was. A light shone in the midst of his moral poverty and despair. His tears of sorrow become tears of joy.

"Who brought this prodigy about, to my constant astonishment, and to my confusion? Once again it is the infinite mercy of my God" (Retreat, December 1814).

At that moment he saw himself as one coming out of the tomb. He experienced a new birth and his life was at last becoming meaningful, a meaningfulness for which he had searched for so long and could not find because, to his own detriment, he had been looking for it outside of God.

Eugene de Mazenod did not see the Cross as something morbid. On the contrary, it was the place where the mercy of a tender, loving God was finally revealed. He is a God who does not want the death of the sinner but that he or she might have life and happiness. The Cross is the triumph of love:

"*It was on Calvary that our divine Savior completed his work of redeeming humanity*" (Letter to his grandmother, September 15, 1809).

The knowledge of God which Eugene acquired on that day was much more than just a cerebral acquaintance. It was deeply heartfelt knowledge. It was a loving experience. The God, whom Eugene had until now thought of as the All-Powerful or maybe the Creator, now took on a human appearance, that of the Crucified, that of a person who had loved him first, whose love is gratuitous, who loves simply because God is Love.

Eugene experienced a God who was not "repulsed" by his dissolute life, a God who had sought him out untiringly, "*as though he could not be happy without him.*" God had taken the risk of revealing himself to Eugene's heart just as he was, complete with the weakness and nakedness displayed on the Cross.

Overwhelmed as he was on that Good Friday, he discovered that there was no happiness without the Cross because no happiness is possible without love. God, who loved him even unto death, became the sole aim and object of his life, his final end. Eugene, in his turn, fell in love with the One who had given his life for his sake:

"*Would to heaven that I had never turned away from that standard of the Cross, from which flow true joy and veritable happiness*" (Retreat, December 1814).

From then onwards his sinfulness became a source of wonder. He discovered the deeper meaning of the words of St. Paul to proclaim that only through the discovery of sin and the truth about one's self can one be led to the discovery of the immensely gratuitous love of the Crucified One:

"*Two streams of tears flow with peace and sweetness and my soul is in such a state of ecstasy that I cannot express it ... if the thought of my sinfulness still comes back to me, it is because love has given it another appearance ...*" (Letter to Mr. Duclaux, December 21, 1811).

Deeply touched as his heart was, Eugene became sufficiently humble to beg for love and for the tenderness and mercy of the Savior:

"*My Lord, my God, my Love, bring me to love you; this only do I ask, for I know full well that this is everything. Give me your love! ... The past is still present to my mind ... but you, O my Savior, do you forget it, and keep in mind only your mercies*" (Retreat Notes, December 1–21, 1811).

If we wish to sum up in one phrase the spirituality of St. Eugene, we may do so by expressing his deep sense of awe in the presence of the Cross. He never ceased to be amazed by this overflowing love manifested by God in his Son Jesus:

"*The more I alienated myself from you, the more you sought me out. You were the tender and pampering father who never tired of supporting and embracing your beloved son*" (Retreat Notes, December 1–21, 1811).

He was surprised by his priestly vocation: "*Who brought about this prodigy, to my constant astonishment and confusion?*" (Retreat, December 1814).

He was also astounded by his vocation as Founder of a Missionary Congregation "*whose only distinctive sign will be the crucified Lord*" (Oblate Rule of 1818).

He was astonished too by his vocation as a preacher whose only mission will be "*to preach Jesus Christ and Jesus Christ crucified*" (Oblate Rule of 1826).

Finally, his astonishment was great at the end of his life, as he calmly watched the approach of death: *"my first thought is to lose myself in thanksgiving before God"* (Last Will and Testament, August 1, 1854).

Every moment of his life, he was wonder-struck in the presence of the Cross of Christ:

"*Yes, my God, I would like to love you as much as you love yourself*" (Retreat Notes, December 1–21, 1811).

A Meditation in the Company of St. Eugene

St. Eugene,

how I too would love to have your Good Friday experience! I too wish to have, once and for all, the enthusiasm inspired by the loving glance of Christ and allow myself to be swept up in the whirlwind engendered by the exchange of glances, in the outstretched arms which express a fidelity which is stronger than death.

Teach me to pause before the Cross so as to get away from the habits and routine of my life.

Teach me to find in the Cross the only meaning of my life because in it love is crystallized, love is hoped for and love is received, love is given in return for love.

Teach me to see the Cross as the mirror which shows me my real face. Not the face of a poor and unfaithful sinner, but the face of one with whom God has fallen in love *"when he wishes his heart to speak to mine."*

Teach me to find the meaning of each day *"by placing everything at the foot of the Cross ... and having peace of mind thereafter"* (Letter to his mother, October 14, 1811).

Teach me to be an enthusiast of the folly of the Cross and to repeat every day: "it is unthinkable that one should be loved so much" and to say as you said in imitation of the Apostle Paul:

"Far be it from me to glory in anything except in the Cross of Our Lord Jesus Christ by which the world has been crucified to me and I to the world" (Gal 6:4).

Reflection Questions

What feelings does the sight of Christ on the cross bring to mind? How does the cross give me strength? What has been my experience of being loved despite my failings? When has my heart been touched by the love God has for me?

3
Discovering
Christ's Friendship

Focus Point

////////////

The loving acceptance involved in a good friendship allows one to feel trust. In that safe environment of trust, I can honestly look at myself and see the areas that need changing. Then, with the support of that friendship, I can move forward in life.

////////////

"Lord Jesus, not only are you my creator and my redeemer as you are of all humanity, but you are also my special benefactor, you are my friend. Yes indeed, you are the friend who has shown me your tenderness in a very special way. You are my generous friend who has chosen to forget all my ingratitude and loved me as intensely as if I had always remained faithful to you. You have carried me upon your shoulders. You have washed my wounds" (Retreat Notes, December 1–21, 1811).

//////////////

*T*hat sums up what impelled Eugene de Mazenod to give his life for Christ. In October 1808, he took a decision which came as a surprise and a shock to his family and friends: he entered the seminary.

His struggle, however, was far from over. Getting rid of one's past is not as easy as that. It cannot be done by merely making a decision, however radical, and especially not if one decides to rely on one's own resources.

Gradually the past tended to resurface. Eugene promised to change, to do better. He took numerous resolutions, undertook severe penances, days of fasting, hours of prayer. The more he added to them, however, the more he realized that he was unable to love as he is loved. He might very well *"cut back the things which are injurious to him, uproot whatever impedes the action of God."* However, he always arrived at the same conclusion: his own efforts were not sufficient for him to love as he is loved.

The moment of truth came at last, one evening in December of 1811, while he was meditating on the parable of the Prodigal Son (Lk 15:11–24). He had become so accustomed to this parable that it was routine to meditate upon it. Now, for the first time, however, it struck him that this was his own story. He was the child who had wandered away and who was now making excuses to his father. He was the son who saw his father's arms outstretched to welcome him home. He was the younger son who had been made the heir by being given the ring, new clothing and the first place at the banquet prepared by his father. Since he was unable to make reparation for the wrong he had done, the prodigal son had to be content to receive his father's embraces. Nothing more was being asked of him.

From the parable of the Prodigal Son, Eugene moved on to that of the sheep that has been lost and found (Jn 10:11–16). The outcome was the same, the story was no different; friendship was bestowed without anything being given in return. From the depths of his soul he exclaimed:

"Not only are you my Creator and my Redeemer, you are also my Benefactor. You are my generous friend and you have chosen to forget my ingratitude by helping me as vigorously as if I had always remained faithful to you. You have borne me on your shoulders. You have made me feel the warmth of your heart. You have washed my wounds" (Retreat Notes, December 1–21, 1811).

Eugene had made a breakthrough. He recognized that everything came from God, that it was given gratuitously and that there was no merit on his part. For the first time he dared to speak of Christ as his Friend. Henceforth he could live under the gaze of his friend, a friend who was watchful and attentive, a friend who was always at his side, a friend who was tender but demanding, a friend in whom he vowed to place his unbounded trust.

He had found in Jesus Christ the friend for whom he had longed: his relationship with Christ became increasingly intimate.

Eugene de Mazenod's relationship with Christ was to be deeply intimate in every moment of his life. For him, an abstract and distant God had become a Person, a loving Being whom he loved, the mainspring of his life, his heart of hearts. Thus, on the evening of his ordination he could write:

"*The thought which strikes me most forcibly and in which I tend to lose myself is this: Jesus has chosen this way to avenge himself of my ingratitude: he has made me his friend, he does everything for me so that, although he is God, he could not do more for me*" (Letter to Mr. Duclaux, December 21, 1811).

From this time onwards he considered any other way of seeing Christ as being a waste of time. When a preacher invited him to meditate on hell he refused most energetically:

"*Why spend in the company of devils the little time left to me to converse with my Master? It is with his love that I wish to fortify myself. I can no longer pay heed to the language of terror. His love alone is acting powerfully in me ... it is love and love alone that must bear the entire cost*" (Retreat Notes, December 1–21, 1811).

His preference was for spending time in silence with his Friend rather than any other act of devotion. In both his joys and sorrows, he "hastens to his feet for refuge." The silence of contemplation and mutual listening had become the key point of each day for him. In the midst of his many activities he always kept a time apart for this heart-to-heart meeting. On one occasion, after a night spent in adoration, he wrote: "*What a beautiful night we have spent there close to this good Master, this adorable Friend.*"

In the deeply moving act of Christ washing the feet of his Apostles, Eugene saw the most eloquent sign of the Lord's friendship for humanity. He could never think of that incident without deep emotion: Christ on his knees before him, a mere man of no substance, and washing his feet while declaring to him: "I no longer call you servant, but my friend."

"*By washing the feet of his disciples, Christ wished the union between creator and creature to be as perfect as it was possible to conceive*" (Lenten Pastoral, 1859).

From this time onwards his whole life was to be stamped with the joy of being in the presence of his Friend. Even when the Friend was silent, even when his presence was so discreet that he seemed absent, Eugene always felt that he was there and he "*experienced sweet emotions,*" "*consolations*" and "*happiness,*" even "*ecstasy*" as though in the presence of a "*fire which warmed and consumed the heart right to its very depths.*"

"This morning, before receiving Communion, I dared to speak to my good Master with the same abandon as I would have done if I had the happiness of living while he was on this earth, and I was in the same predicament as I am today.... I made known our needs, I asked for light and assistance, and then I abandoned myself entirely to the Lord, not wishing for anything other than God's holy will.... I was at ease, I was happy, I felt loving and grateful" (Letter to Fr. Tempier, August 23, 1830).

A Meditation in the Company of St. Eugene

St. Eugene,

just as you did, I also try to get there of my own accord. Each time I go to confession, I firmly resolve not to offend Christ again. Each time I make a retreat, I undertake to do better on one or other point. And then I fall again.

Since you have known the same problems and the same setbacks, since it took you so many years before daring to say to Christ those simple words: "my Friend," be my guide on this path of shedding my own will.

Here I am at the Savior's feet: show me the path that will allow me to pass from a world of merit and recompense to that of gratuitous giving.

"Christ is the God of mercy who came among us only to call sinners. It is to them that his most loving words are addressed. He seeks them out, he presses them

against his heart. He carries them upon his shoulders" (Retreat Resolutions, October 12, 1808).

Then I, in my turn, will be able to hear in the depths of my heart the voice which murmurs:

"It is my wish that my joy may be in you and your joy may be complete....

"I no longer call you servant, because a servant does not know what his master is doing.

"I call you my friend....

"It was not you who chose me, but I who chose you ..." (Jn 15:11–16).

Reflection Questions

Which of my friendships are both encouraging and call me to accountability? How does my relationship with God (my Higher Power) bring joy to my life? In what ways have my friendships changed from what they were 10 years ago? How do people see me as a friend?

4
Working
for the Glory of God

Focus Point

//////////////

Each person is called to do the will of God. My circumstances are different from Eugene de Mazenod's, but my talents are needed to build up this world. Within the context of my work and relationships I need to discover what God wants me to do.

//////////////

"What more glorious occupation than to act in everything and to do everything only for the glory of God, to love him above all else, and to love God all the more because I was late in beginning to love him at all! Indeed, this is to begin already on this earth the blessed life of heaven" (Retreat, December 1814).

//////////////

*H*aving been ordained a priest on December 21, 1811, Eugene de Mazenod returned to his native diocese of Aix in October, 1812. The question he now asked himself was: what type of ministry did he wish to undertake? The only thing he felt certain about was that, whatever ministry he might accept, it would have to be for the glory of God:

"My God, you have given me intelligence, will, memory, a heart, eyes, hands, in a word all my bodily senses, all my soul's faculties; you gave me all these things for yourself, to use them for your glory, for your unique, your great glory. My God, I have now decided that henceforth for the rest of my life, you and you alone will be the sole object to which will tend all my affections and my every act. To please you, to act for your glory will be my daily task, the task of every moment of my life. It is my wish to live for you alone and that all else should be in you and for you" (Retreat Notes, December 1–21, 1811).

The glory of the Father! That expression is repeated on almost every page. But what does Eugene really mean by it? To understand it we must contemplate Jesus Christ, passionately devoted to his Father, totally concentrated on his Father. His purpose in coming into the world was to do the will of his Father and to accomplish it perfectly by dying on the Cross: "Father, glorify your Son so that your Son may glorify you!" (Jn 17:1).

By allowing himself to be loved by Jesus Christ and trying to love him with his whole being in return, his feelings naturally became those of Jesus Christ. Passionately devoted to the Lord, he wished to imitate him who had become his Friend and his Model:

"Not having imitated my Model in his innocence, may I be permitted to imitate him in his dedication to the glory of his Father?" (Spiritual Conference, March 19, 1809).

The whole of Eugene's spirituality, therefore, is based on adopting this attitude of the Son who accomplishes the will of his Father. He tried to make it his own attitude, to realize it in his own life and to draw strength and energy from it in all circumstances.

In 1813, it is because *"he seeks only the glory of God"* that he founded a clandestine society for youth, those young people who *"have been reared to recognize no other God but Napoleon."*

In 1815, in his letter to Fr. Tempier inviting him to join him in the parish missions venture, he asked him to read the letter *"at the foot of the cruci-fix, and disposed to listen to God alone and the demands which God's glory requires of a priest such as he."*

In 1816, it was because *"the sight of the evils which have brought about the de-christianization of the countryside has touched the hearts of certain priests who are zealous for the glory of God"* that he set up what was to become the Congregation of the Missionary Oblates of Mary Immaculate.

In 1825, the reason he sought approval in Rome for his newly born religious family was *"so that it may do all the good dependent on it but only do it for the glory of God."*

In 1826, when the Pope approved the Oblates, Eugene drew the conclusion *"that he must now work with even more ardor and more absolute dedication to procure God's glory insofar as it depended on him."*

In 1841, it was because *"the only thing he wanted was God's glory"* that he launched the Congregation on missions outside France by sending six missionaries to Canada.

The list could be continued right up to the time of his death.

In all of his spiritual life and in all his pastoral activities, Eugene de Mazenod developed his quest for the glory of God in four directions.

First of all, he wished to be an imitator of Jesus Christ: *"I now see the Model whom I must imitate, the living example which I must follow."* The very being of Christ is the accomplishment of the will of the Father and the realization of his glory: "He who seeks the glory of him who sent him is true" (Jn 7:18). In his desire to imitate the Lord, Eugene's life could only be an impassioned search for the will of the Father and its accomplishment in all things and in all times and places.

Secondly, he was a man, a priest, a bishop who was totally free. Just as Christ was free with respect to everyone else because the only law which bound him was the will of his Father, so Eugene abandoned the constraints of his social class and those of the moralizing practices of the Jansenist church of his time. He was sufficiently free to preach in Provençal, sufficiently free to show his independence of the various political powers, sufficiently free to be guided by love alone, because "*our only duty, the essential thing in our life is to please God.*"

Thirdly, he radiated a great interior peace. Jesus experienced in his human heart the horror of abandonment which is the Cross: "Now my soul is troubled and what shall I say? 'Father, save me from this hour?' No, for this purpose I have come to this hour. Father, glorify your name." (Jn 12:27–28). Since his heart was at peace, Jesus could proclaim that victory is certain: "When I have been raised up from the earth, I shall draw all to me" (Jn 12:32). There was no lack of trials in Eugene's life and his sensitive heart always suffered enormously from them. But nothing ever disturbed his peace of mind. In one of the darkest of those moments he would exclaim:

"*The only compensation for my trouble is to see that God is glorified by it. Provided he is praised, what does it matter if I am humiliated, neglected and abandoned by almost everybody?*" (Letter to Bishop Frezza, April 27, 1835).

Finally, it is in the search for the glory of the Father that we may find the roots of Eugene's apostolic zeal. Here too, all he did was imitate Jesus Christ who came into the world, not to do his own will, but the will of him who sent him. It was the will of the one who sent him that he should not lose one of those whom the Father had given him (Jn 6:38–39). In imitation of Christ, Eugene always linked the glory of God to the salvation of human beings.

By nature, he tended to live his friend-ship with Christ in a cozy spiritual intimacy, enclosed, as it were, in a cocoon and sheltered from worldly contingencies:

"I long for solitude, and I feel attracted by the reli-gious orders whose only concern for others is in their prayers" (Letter to Fr. de Janson, September 12, 1814).

His passionate longing for God's glory, how-ever, forced him out of his cocoon: *"so that the Father's name may be known and blessed"* and that it may be *"adored from one end of the earth to the other."*

"I do all that I have to do. God will do the rest. We live only for him. All we wish for is the glory of his holy name and the salvation of the souls whom he has redeemed. When we have used all the means in our power, we should be at peace and not be worried about anything" (Letter to Fr. Tempier, June 10, 1826).

A Meditation in the Company of St. Eugene

St. Eugene,

each day I repeat in my prayer the words: "Our Father ... hallowed be Thy name...."

If only I could imitate Jesus Christ to the extent that I could make his impassioned love for the Father mine, to the extent that my only desire would be the glory of the Father and the fulfillment of his will!

If only I could be seriously willing to make a success of my life, to make it fruitful! Then, under your guidance, Eugene, I would be mindful of the Father's glory, I would be united with the Son and I would make way in my heart for the Spirit who murmurs: "Abba, Father."

If only I could be daring for my own good, daring enough to do what God wants me to do, daring enough to experience the indulgent care of God!

"Heavenly Father, make yourself known as God, make your kingdom come, make your will be done on earth as it is in heaven" (Mt 6:9–10).

Reflection Questions

How do I seek to do the will of God? When have I felt like I was doing the will of God? When have I experienced inner peace despite encountering difficulties? How do my work and my relationships help to bring about a better world?

5
Option for Humanity

Focus Point

////////////

Created in the image of God, I am precious in God's sight. There is a freedom in believing this is true. Knowing how valuable I am in the eyes of God leads me to work for the dignity of others, especially those who are most in need.

////////////

" *D uring this holy season of Lent, there will be an abundance of instructions for the rich, for people who have received an education, but will there be any for the poor and the unlettered? The poor, a precious portion of the Christian family, cannot be abandoned to their ignorance.... After all what is at issue here? You, the poor, the needy, whom the injustice of men obliges to beg for the bread which will sustain your existence. The world sees you as the rejects of society.... But you, the poor of Jesus Christ, you are oppressed by misery, my dear people, my very dear and respectable people, listen to me: you are the children of God, the heirs of his eternal kingdom, you are the chosen portion of God's inheritance"* (Ash Wednesday Homily, March 3, 1813).

On Ash Wednesday, March 3, 1813, the upper classes of Aix were up in arms: Father de Mazenod, the son of the President of the Court, had been preaching in Provençal, the language of the people, to the domestics, the farm laborers, the poor of all sorts. And what a sermon! Did he not go so far as to say to them:

"Who are you in the eyes of the world? A class of slaves to those who pay your wages, exposed to the disdain, the injustice and even the ill treatment of your masters who think they have bought the right to be unjust to you with the paltry wages they pay you!" (Ash Wednesday Homily, March 3, 1813).

That was not the only thing he had done. He had shown his freedom in the eyes of the comfortable by accompanying to the guillotine a worthless woman named Germaine, declaring that she was *"worthy of admiration because the Lord had shed his blood for her also."* Besides, he had gathered together a group of young people who were wandering the streets and who were most abandoned in their ways *"so as to try to save them from the evils which threatened them."*

Had he lost his head? No! He was merely carrying to the limit the discovery which had shaken his existence on that Good Friday in 1807, when he was enlightened by the love of

God for humanity. By choosing God as the center of his life, he had chosen the human beings whom the Father had made to his own image and likeness, the human beings for whom the Son had given his life on the Cross, the human beings who had been called to become temples of the Holy Spirit:

"Called by my vocation to be the servant and priest of humanity, especially of the poor, to whose service I would like to be able to devote my whole life" (Lenten Homily, March 28, 1813).

His first inclination to seek enclosure in spiritual intimacy with God had been brushed aside by meeting with those other people whom nobody wanted, those who counted for nothing in the eyes of the world, the most abandoned. His docility to the will of the Father had urged him: *"to take over the mission of the Beloved One,"* to walk in his footsteps, *"to become the co-worker with the Savior and the co-redeemer of the human race."* To his ardent desire for the glory of God he could now add his zeal for the salvation of humanity which was equally ardent. The desire for both these ends became the one and only desire in his life.

"I must, above all, become really convinced that I am doing the will of God by devoting myself to the service of my neighbor ... and then I must do my best, without worrying if, in doing work of this kind, I am unable to do other things which I would

perhaps find more to my taste and which would seem more adapted to my own sanctification. If, at some time when I feel attracted to contemplate the mercies of Jesus Christ in the Holy Sacrament, and I am called upon to do a work of charity, I must, without murmur or regret, leave the presence of Our Lord to perform this duty imposed upon me by his will...." (Retreat, July-August 1816).

His option for human beings is above all a preferential option to work for the good of men and women created in the image of God. It is not merely a question of doing works of charity but of revealing human beings to themselves, showing them who they are in the eyes of God.

"We shall begin by telling you who you are, informing you of your noble origin and the rights which it bestows upon you as well as the obligations which it imposes....

"Men and women are creatures of God, and you, you are God's children, the brothers and sisters of Jesus Christ.... You are kings, you are priests, you are, in a way, gods.... Within each of you there is an immortal soul made in the image of God whom it is destined one day to possess, a soul which has been redeemed at the cost of the blood of Christ.... God alone is worthy of your soul. Only God can satisfy your heart" (Ash Wednesday Homily, March 3, 1813).

Having discovered how valuable he was in the sight of God, Eugene de Mazenod burned with a desire to reveal to each and every human being their eminent dignity. That was the way he chose to go; henceforth, his attention turned to the lives of men and women.

His meeting with the domestic servants made this young man of noble rank break away from his monastic tendencies and launch out into the Lenten sermons given in the Church of the Madeleine, sermons which seemed so scandalous in the eyes of the world.

His encounter with the miserable conditions of the country people and the agricultural workers made this young city dweller go out beyond the city walls and take to the roads of Provence.

His meeting with those condemned to death and despised by all made this lawyer's son jostle the prevailing morality and discover a spark of the divine in the most criminal.

Because Eugene saw them as the children of God, he had a band of socially unacceptable youths take the place of honor in the center of the Aix cathedral on the day of their Confirmation, in the presence of the canons who were scandalized by it all.

Because they were children of God, he received the fishwives of Marseille's Old Harbor in the office of his episcopal residence, while the Mayor of the city waited in the antechamber.

Because the sick were worthy of God's care, he left an official luncheon in his honor to bring the last Sacraments to an old drunken lady in the most disreputable area of Marseille.

Because those afflicted by the plague were precious in the eyes of God he besieged the civil administration until he obtained permission to go and help them.

"I will make every effort to be indifferent as to matters of health and sickness, to good or bad reputation, riches or poverty, honors or disgrace, not desiring and willing anything at all, except what the glory of God and the salvation of souls might require me to do" (Retreat Notes, December 1–21, 1811).

Faithful to the zealous desire of St. Eugene for God and for human beings, the Oblates of today give expression in their Constitutions and Rules to the unique option they make for the glory of God and the salvation of souls: "Through the eyes of our crucified Savior we see the world which he redeemed with his blood, desiring that those in whom he continues to suffer will also know the power of his resurrection" (Oblate Rule of 2000).

A Meditation in the Company of St. Eugene

St. Eugene,

the unconditional option for human beings is one which holds great attraction because it means entering into the love of the other person. I shall never have enough of love. I shall never reach the end of love. I shall never know just how far it can lead me.

"The one who says, 'I love God,' and does not love a fellow human being, is a liar" (1 Jn 4:20).

The preferential option for human beings is attractive because it means that I no longer care what people say and I no longer tend to wrap the other person in my own fixed ideas but that now I see that person with the eyes of Christ.

"The one who says, 'I love God,' and does not love a fellow human being, is a liar" (1 Jn 4:20).

The unconditional option for human beings is attractive, because there are persons who cause me to despair, so much do they seem beyond redemption.

"The one who says, 'I love God,' and does not love a fellow human being, is a liar" (1 Jn 4:20).

Reflection Questions

I am precious to God; do I believe that even when the world says otherwise? How do I work for the good of others? Am I willing to risk ridicule by helping those who are on the margins of society? If I am not able to go out to do mission work, can I support those who do by my prayers and financial support?

6
At the Service
of the Church

/////////////

Eugene saw the defects and problems in the Church and loved it anyway. Instead of complaining about the situation, he sought to help the Church fulfill its mission: strengthening the weak and caring for its members.

/////////////

"How could it be possible to separate our love for Jesus Christ from that which we must have for his Church? These two loves are inseparable: to love the Church is to love Jesus Christ and vice versa. We love Jesus Christ in his Church because the Church is his immaculate spouse which came from his side on the Cross" (Lenten Pastoral, 1860).

/////////////

*A*cting as he did, free of institutions and principles, Eugene irritated the Archbishop and the parish priests of Aix. Who did this know-it-all think he was by trying to teach them lessons about pastoral approach? Is he not setting up his own institution independently of the Church? Accusations began to multiply, including that of refusing to be at the service of the Church.

In the face of these calumnies, Eugene kept his calm. The Church was at the heart of his ministry. In fact, the reason he had become a priest was to place himself humbly at the service of the Church:

"*I saw the Church being threatened by the most cruel persecution.... Therefore I entered the seminary with a desire, nay with the determination, to dedicate myself in the most absolute manner to the service of the Church*" (Diary, 1846).

Having become a priest in order to answer "*the call of the divine Master to serve the Church at a time when she was being abandoned by all,*" he accepted whatever the Church required of him. It was because "*it is unbecoming for a son to disobey his mother*" that he accepted to become Vicar General of Marseille in 1823. The reason he accepted to become bishop in 1832 was "*to share in the solicitude of the Church and to make a still greater contribution to bringing back to the Church those of her children who have gone astray.*"

Impassioned for the glory of God and impassioned also for the salvation of human beings,

Eugene de Mazenod was equally zealous for the Church. He took as his motto: *"All for the glory of God, for the service of the Church and the salvation of souls."*

He had an ardent love for the Church as he had an intense love for Christ because the Church *"is the spouse washed and purified in the blood of the Cross,"* the first fruit of the loving Passion of God for humanity. He loved the Church, as it was, with its defects and faults. He regretted the Church's slowness, its routine and its timidity but he loved it because it was born from the open wound in Christ's side and because it was therefore his Mother.

Because of his impassioned love for the Church he wanted it to be more beautiful, more radiant, more dynamic and active, more attentive to telling people who Christ is, reaching out ever more beyond its boundaries. He felt unable to share in what he saw as its slothfulness, its intolerance or its tepidity:

"The salvation of souls is our special vocation. It is the work towards which all efforts should be directed, and the accidents permitted by God should not be allowed to hinder the supernatural progress of that work. We should not hold back in the face of anything except sin. Everything else must be overcome because of the excellence of the purpose at which we are aiming" (Letter to Bishop de Forbin-Janson, December 11, 1835).

It was his passionate love of the Church which caused him to be shocked by the state of ruin in which he found it after the Revolution and the Empire. His burning desire was to raise it up again so that once again it might appear "*beautiful and spotless in the presence of the bridegroom.*"

It was because of his fervent love for the Church that he was saddened at seeing so many Christians desert it and he wished to devote his whole life to bringing them back to the sheepfold of the one and only Pastor:

"*The Church, that glorious inheritance purchased by Christ the Savior at the cost of his own blood, has in our days been cruelly ravaged. Faced with such a deplorable situation the Church earnestly appeals to the ministers whom she herself enrolled in the cause of her divine Spouse*" (Oblate Rule of 1818).

Love of Christ and love of his Church were the sap which nourished the life of St. Eugene. From the beginning, the two loves were fused together in him. As his love for Christ increased, so also did his love for the Church and vice versa.

The Church was the one and only place where Eugene de Mazenod's love of Christ developed and became the ultimate aim of his life. That was why he considered it so important that the Church should be spread to the ends of the earth. His aim in accomplishing that mission was not inspired by a spirit of triumphalism but by his desire to ensure that every human being should have access to Christ:

"*We have all been baptized in the same spirit; the only reason why we are together with him is because we are all members of the Church*" (Lenten Pastoral, 1846).

Moreover, the Church was for him the Mystical Body of Christ and from the time of his entry into the seminary he rejoiced at the idea that he was "*a member of this great family of which God himself is the head.*" Every Christian was a member of this body which meant that each one lived with the life of Christ himself and that each one was equal in dignity to all the others and that all had equal obligations and each one had a place to maintain:

"*We are all members of the same body, the Church; each one contributes through his or her efforts, and sacrifices, if necessary, to the well-being of the body and the development of all its faculties*" (Letter to Fr. Honorat, October 9, 1841).

Writing to an Oblate in France who was straining at the leash to join his "missionary" brothers in their exploits, Eugene reminded him of the unity which exists among all those who work for the spread of the Gospel:

"*Let us rejoice together at the good which others are doing for the Church. To sum it all up: we are in solidarity with one another. Each one is working for all and all for each one*" (Letter to Fr. Baudrand, January 11, 1850).

Finally, it was in the Church that the perfect union of human beings among themselves was already being realized. In the Church, Christ's commandment to his disciples to love one another was already effective. The members of the Church bore one another's burdens, they suffered for one another, they rejoiced with one another because *"in the Church we should love one another as children of the same father and there should be no exception whether of persons or nations."*

For Eugene de Mazenod, the Church was, in the last analysis, *"the Mother of all Christians. Its mission was "to watch over them carefully from the cradle to the grave."*

He used incredibly tender words to describe the Church: *"She raises her children who have fallen. She strengthens them when they are weak. She enlightens them in their doubts."* Above all: *"she causes them to share in the spiritual riches which the divine Spouse has entrusted to her as a treasure to be dispensed."*

"Christ has identified with our cause to the extent of identifying himself with us. Thus he is the Spouse of the Church and the Church is his mystical body" (Lenten Pastoral, 1846).

A Meditation in the Company of St. Eugene

St. Eugene,

I am deeply impressed by your intense love for the Church and your desire to make the Church loved.

I am inspired by the fact that instead of deserting the Church you committed yourself to working for its revival.

I am moved by the way you reminded the Church that it must never forget the poor and the most abandoned.

I am touched by your reminder to me that I have a place to be maintained within the Church.

I am encouraged by your recognition that the Church is your Mother and simply because of that, you had to love it.

Therefore, St. Eugene, teach me to love the Church as you loved it. Teach me to serve it as you served it, only for the glory of God and for the happiness of human beings.

"The God of Our Lord Jesus Christ has put all things beneath his feet and made him the head of all things for the church, which is his body, the fullness of the one who fills all things in every way" (Eph 1:22–23).

Reflection Questions

What helps me remain calm during difficult situations? In what ways have people welcomed me to be part of the Church? How is it possible to love the Church with its defects and faults? How can I be of service to the Church?

7

Daring to Strive
for Holiness

Focus Point

////////////

To aspire to be a saint seems an impossible task,
especially if God is viewed as a harsh judge. God
doesn't wait to come to us when we are perfect,
God comes to us amid our sinful nature and calls
us to holiness.

////////////

*"Know your dignity.... In the name of God be
saints"* (Letter to Fr. Tempier, February 18, 1826).

////////////

*T*his little phrase, a sort of punch line, was
an often repeated refrain flowing from
the pen of Eugene de Mazenod. The very tone
of it rang like a challenge in a Church tainted
by Jansenism where people looked upon them-

selves only as sinners, unworthy and incapable of raising their eyes towards the One who is the All Holy.

The invitation to holiness was addressed first of all to himself. It was with the intention of becoming a saint that he decided *"to live among the saints"* on entering the seminary.

He addressed the same invitation to those whom he invited to join him in religious life:

"The Oblates must devote themselves seriously to becoming saints ... live with the constant intention of reaching perfection" (Oblate Rule of 1818).

It is an invitation which he extended to all baptized persons and which he set as the aim of every work of evangelization:

"(Our mission is to lead people) *to act like human beings, first of all, and then like Christians, and finally, we must help them to become saints"* (Oblate Rule of 1818).

He extended the invitation even to the most hardened sinners, the worst criminals, by addressing to everybody the words:

"Be saints."

We may well ask: what is this saintliness of which he spoke and which we so easily leave aside by saying that it concerns only a few exceptional people but could not be intended for us?

Holiness is not a condition or state. On the contrary, it is a path to be followed, a way forward, a dynamic. The saints are not only those who have reached the end of the road but also those who accept to undertake the journey. That is why the sight of our sinfulness should not discourage us but should instead give new dynamism to our desire for holiness:

"Never be discouraged when one commits a fault, but humble oneself immediately, without fretting, and turn to God with an act of contrition, renewing one's good intention not to sin again; then recover one's peace of soul; and do likewise each time one falls, even if it be one hundred times a day" (Personal Notes, 1809).

For Eugene de Mazenod, the call to sanctity was at the meeting place of two wills: the will of God and the will of the human being. In the first place, it was God's desire that each human being should share in his own unique holiness. Then the human being willed to adhere to this plan and make it his or her own. God took the initiative. God came in search of the human being, knocking at the door, and then calling by name. The state of holiness into which God would have us enter was not a condition of mere sinlessness but a dynamic and loving relationship.

"In the matter of holiness, we must never say: that is enough" (Act of Visitation, Billens, August 26, 1831).

The young Count de Mazenod was impassioned by his own person and by his financial and amorous successes, but then he discovered that he was called to holiness because God had looked lovingly upon him.

For him, becoming a saint became the logical consequence of choosing to follow and imitate Jesus Christ. The position he adopted with regard to Christ was that of an artist wishing to make a copy of his model. Christ was *"the lovable model who must be imitated if one wishes to become a saint."*

When Eugene de Mazenod ceased wanting to fulfill his own desires, when he ceased wanting to build his life according to his own criteria for success and when he finally got around to wanting what God wanted, when his criteria for success became God's plan for him, he had already begun to become a saint.

Becoming a saint means wanting what God wants for us, it means daring to enter into the desire for holiness which God has for each one of us. The human being is truly great in the eyes of God and is lowered in dignity each time he or she refuses to be lifted up to the level of one's calling.

One of the great novelties which St. Eugene contributed to the spirituality of that era was his desire to promote this holiness for everybody and to let everybody know that he or she was invited to pursue it.

He issued the invitation to each one of his sons, the Missionary Oblates and he did so with words of fire:

"Burn with the desire to become saints!"

He also issued the invitation to his sister, Ninette, when he wrote to her that marriage is as much a way of holiness as religious life:

"We must become saints in whatever calling we may be ... a married woman is called to holiness just as an unmarried lady or a religious" (Letter to Mrs. de Boisgelin, April 1809).

He also addressed the invitation to the neglected masses of Aix and he aroused their enthusiasm by revealing to them that *"Only God is worthy of them."*

The invitation to become holy became the unifying principle of his life. His primary concern was neither preaching, nor prayer, nor silence, nor charitable works, but the imitation of Jesus Christ in each one of his everyday actions, whatever they might be, in order to become holy as He alone is holy.

His search for holiness did not cut him off from the world. On the contrary, it moved him to go out to the world. Quite simply, it was in the conditions in which he lived and among the persons and situations he encountered that he undertook this journey to holiness. He chose to reach out to human beings as Christ reached out to them, to turn to the Father as Christ turned to him, to accept whatever happened as Christ accepted it:

"Never allow yourself to be defeated by the contradictions and sufferings which are an inevitable part of our existence whatever may be the conditions in which we find ourselves. Wisdom lies in taking advantage of all things to advance in holiness" (Letter to Fr. Végreville, April 17, 1860).

Sanctity was not acquired independently of others. Christians could become saints together, linked to one another by mutual love. Being a saint meant living Christ fully and allowing one's self to be transformed by the Spirit whom he places within us:

"*Let us be united in the love of Christ. In our common search for holiness let us love one another and be united in our work*" (Letter to Fr. Courtès, March 3, 1822).

We cannot become saints except by becoming so with one another and leading one another along as we undertake this prodigious adventure.

On becoming Bishop of Marseille, Eugene de Mazenod began by proclaiming that he wished to become a good bishop. He proceeded to define what being a good bishop meant:

"*In a word, by working effectively for the sanctification of my flock, I wish to sanctify myself to an eminent degree of perfection*" (Retreat Notes, May 1837).

A person did not become a saint for his or her own sake, in order to have personal satisfaction or to obtain a place in paradise. A saint became a saint with others and for others. Saints were made by advancing God's loving plan for the world.

"*Become saints and then you will build up the Church*" (Circular Letter No. 1, August 2, 1853).

A Meditation in the Company
of St. Eugene

St. Eugene,

I do not wish to be disrespectful with regard to those whom the Church has canonized but I am sometimes inclined to think that you were completely crazy!

You were foolish when, after the life you have lived, you pretended that you were called to be a saint. Yours, however, is the folly of Jesus when he told that rogue Zacchaeus: "Come down quickly, this day I shall dine in your house!" (Lk 19:5).

You were imprudent when you embraced those condemned to death, saying that they "*were predestined to holiness.*" That too is the folly of Jesus, when he told the bandit who had been crucified with him: "This day you will be with me in paradise!" (Lk 23:43).

You were crazy when you called to sanctity the undesirable youths who were loitering in the streets of Aix; but then yours was the folly of Jesus when he chose his apostles, not all of whom were to be reputable.

You were foolish but yours was the folly of God and I would indeed wish to have just a little of that folly in my own life.

I would like to have some of your folly so that I could discover that there are also others who are called to that sanctity and that I could reveal it to them when they are uncertain of themselves. With just a little of that folly I would:

"... have strength to comprehend with all the holy ones what is the breadth and length and height and depth, and to know the love of Christ that surpasses knowledge, so that I may be filled with all the fullness of God" (Eph 3:18–19).

Reflection Questions

How would I describe my present image of God; and the image of God I held as a child? What human qualities do I admire in good people? When have I been successful in overcoming a fault? What changes do I need to make in my life to choose the path of holiness?

8

Daring to Break
away from Routine

Focus Point

To take care of those in need, is more important
than how well we follow the rules. God is inter-
ested in our love, not our laws. Especially for those
in leadership, it is their duty to seek out and help
those who are suffering.

//////////////

"*Everything is done by routine. The important
thing is to change nothing, that is, one must do as
little and as badly as those who came before; ordinary
humdrum suffices. But surely that is a mercenary
way to work. Should the chief pastor tolerate such
abuses...? We must move forward. Of necessity, this
is what God is imposing upon me. Let us be courageous and count upon his grace. In order to do so,
I must work seriously at trying to become a saint*"
(Retreat Notes, May 1837).

//////////////

*A*fter his ordination, Eugene de Mazenod worked out a program for himself in which he left nothing to chance. His days were carefully planned and his meetings with people were reduced to a strict minimum:

"Every moment that is not employed in prayer, study or the exercise of the sacred ministry would be time stolen from Him to whose service I have dedicated myself totally.... My whole way of life has been thought out in advance, and nothing will make me change it" (Letter to Mrs. de Mazenod, April 22, 1812).

In following Christ, however, what counts are not great principles or customs, nor even rules, but the men and women who have to be served and loved.

When he took stock of the de-christianization of the countryside in February, 1816, he abandoned his well-regulated lifestyle and set out on the adventure of parish missions. For Eugene, these were the principal instruments which would enable the most abandoned of the flock to encounter the Christ who loves them.

Realizing that the language these people understood was Provençal, he saw to it that all his preaching was done in that language, no matter what the "nice people" might think, and he obliged his collaborators to do the same:

"You have performed an act of cowardice by giving in to the wishes of five or six bourgeois and giving the instructions in French" (Letter to Fr. Honorat, February 28, 1837).

During those missions, he invented liturgies which meant something to the people. He re-introduced the renewal of baptismal promises and had the people sing popular hymns in which all could join. He established reconciliation offices, enabling people to settle charitably the disputes arising from state property sales.

He got away from routine in the matter of confession. Without making light of sin, he gave more serious consideration to the repentant sinner. Contrary to the established practice of making the penitent come back again and again to confession before receiving absolution, he took account of the sincerity of the contrite sinner and consequently did not refuse the sacramental absolution. As though God would have refused his pardon!

"We are the ministers of Christ's mercy. Let us always have the heart of a father.... We, in our ministry, must not only reconcile sinners, we must admit them to the sacred banquet. We must give them the bread of life so that their lives may be renewed" (Letter to Fr. Guigues, February 8, 1837).

On becoming Bishop of Marseille, he realized that his people were totally ignorant of the Lord. So he set about introducing innovations in his homilies during his pastoral visits and his rounds of Confirmation. He spoke neither of the Commandments nor of hell but centered his teaching on Christ. He composed, for the whole diocese, a new catechism which spoke essentially of God's love for humanity:

"The words of the catechism are taught and learned in a dull and half-hearted way but there is little effort to emphasize the goodness of God, the infinite love of Our Lord Jesus Christ for human beings. Nothing is done to form the heart" (Roman Diary, September 13, 1837).

For Eugene, God is not bound by laws or by truths to be believed. God is bound only by a love for men and women, a love which surpasses all rules, customs and sacraments.

When the French army had taken the city of Constantine in Algeria, the bishops refused to hold a service for the soldiers who had fallen in combat because "they almost certainly did not die in the state of grace." Eugene de Mazenod, on the other hand, did not even wait for the Government orders to take the initiative:

"I shall pray and offer the Holy Sacrifice for all soldiers who have fallen on the battlefield or elsewhere. God is infinitely merciful. No one has the right to measure, much less restrain God's mercy" (Roman Diary, October 23, 1837).

Eugene was also innovative in works of charity. During the four epidemics of cholera which ravaged his episcopal city "he took the initiative of providing whatever relief he could for the sick." He held a meeting of religious superiors in the bishop's house and ordered them to establish clinics to dispense medicine, while the Mayor of the city refused to do anything. When the worst of the epidemic had passed, he was once again innovative. He provided for orphans, widows and survivors who had been reduced to misery. He also issued a severe condemnation of the way in which funds, intended for works of charity, had been misappropriated by the city offices:

"Nobody has seen any good effects of the 50,000 Francs which the Mayor's office claims to have distributed.... Meanwhile the poor come streaming to the bishop's house and we have been reduced to selling our blankets to help them" (Roman Diary, September 7, 1837).

Such declarations did not always win him friends but he did not care. In record time he set up orphanages and workshops to train apprentices. He found work for widows and complained bitterly about the sluggishness of *"those who are custom-bound by their habits, because charity simply will not wait."*

"I will have to do battle with egoism, self-interest, lack of zeal, routine, the inaction of leaders.... All of that will not be accomplished without contradictions.... No doubt the cry will be raised when an effort is made to go ahead because reform is never accomplished without ruffling the feathers of many. What matter! All we must have in mind is God, the honor of the Church and the salvation of souls. One must nevertheless abound in virtue to sacrifice one's rest and the duties of state in order to do good for people" (Retreat Notes, May 1837).

A Meditation in the Company
of St. Eugene

St. Eugene,

you did not set yourself up in a ready-made Church just to continue doing what had been done yesterday and the day before. You wanted to go out to those who were outside.

Teach me to have some of your enthusiasm so that I too may learn to get away, to get out of my routine and to want to go further still.

You did not accept uncritically the ideas, laws and principles of your time. You preferred to see human beings with the eyes of Christ.

Teach me to have your enthusiasm so that I too may have your impassioned love for human beings.

You did not accept the ready-made images of God prevalent in your time. You dared to reveal a God who is full of tenderness and mercy.

Teach me to have your enthusiasm so I too may show the loving face of God.

"I know your works, your toil and your patient endurance....

"Yet I hold this against you: you have lost the love you had at first. Repent, and do the works you did at first" (Rev 2:2–5).

Reflection Questions

When have I been willing to leave my routine and help someone in need? What image(s) would you use to explain the mercy of God? When have I experienced someone willing to break from "the rules" and offer me compassion? In what ways do I need to battle egoism, self-interest and lack of enthusiasm?

9
Daring
to Love Others

Focus Point

////////////

Each person is made in the image of God and therefore, loved and cherished by God. Christian love knows no religious boundaries. Following the example of Jesus, this love calls each of us to love all people and serve them in their daily needs.

////////////

"I do not understand how anyone can love God if they do not know how to love human beings. I do not try to hide or disown the sentiments which are mine. On the contrary, I have every reason to thank God for having given me a spirit capable of loving human beings and thus understand the spirit of Jesus Christ my Master. I have little faith in the judgment of those cold and egotistical intellectuals, who apparently locate the heart in the brain, and do not know how to love anyone, except in the last

analysis, they love only themselves" (Roman Diary,
September 4, 1837).

//////////////

*E*ugene de Mazenod disturbed the customs of his time by daring to get away
from routine. He also disturbed a cautious and
Jansenistic Church by daring to let his feelings be known and saying that a person who is
Christian has a heart which is made to love.

He was impressed by the open side of Christ
on the Cross, and in the pierced heart of the
Savior he found the justification of his outra-
geous love for human beings.

*"The Feast of the Sacred Heart is the feast of the
love of Jesus Christ for humanity. Therefore, we must
love others in the strength of the love of Jesus Christ"*
(Spiritual Conference, June 30, 1811).

In was from the Heart of Christ, forever
open, that he drew his intense love for the poor-
est and the most abandoned. He loved the most
neglected precisely because they were unloved,
because they were alone, or had been left aside,
because nobody looked tenderly upon them.

*"It is no trouble to give money but to find one's
self face-to-face with such unfortunate beings and
feeling that it is impossible to meet all their needs,
that is more than I can manage.... I just can't keep
going"* (Diary, September 5, 1838).

On becoming bishop of Marseille, he threw
himself into the work of re-founding his diocese,

building churches, establishing parishes, bringing in religious Congregations, opening schools, initiating charitable works, ceaselessly uniting the bodies and souls of his flock. In the midst of all that he remained in close touch with his people, giving Confirmation to the dying, bringing consolation to the sick, whether known or unknown, visiting families in mourning:

"*I visited a person who is ill with cholera. My visit did that person a world of good and was very edifying for the doctor who arrived at the house of the sick person at the same time as I did. If one only realized what a Bishop really is, there would be less wonder at seeing him approach his flock when they are in trouble or when they are sick or dying*" (Roman Diary, September 8, 1837).

He mourned the death of Lamberte, an excellent woman, devoted to the care of the Oblate community in Calvaire. When someone hinted to him that such an attitude was unworthy of a bishop, he replied:

"*Self-centered persons horrify me, their hearts are insensitive and they see only their own interests and never give anything for what they have received. The more I study the heart of Jesus Christ, the more I meditate on his actions and his precious life, the more I am convinced that I am right and they are wrong*" (Roman Diary, September 2, 1837).

"The people of Marseille speak with admiration of his zeal and his goodness towards the sick and the poor. He never hesitated to go himself and bring help to the needy in the most infamous streets and often he went there to bring the sacraments to the most notorious sinners. His zeal and charity were often spoken of in conversations in the city" (Minutes from the Cause of Beatification).

"*Yes, I love with true, sincere and tender affection.... I thank the Lord for giving me this light, and a soul capable of understanding and appreciating these things*" (Roman Diary, September 2, 1837).

His concern for the welfare of persons led him to extend his efforts well beyond religious boundaries and to serve them in their daily lives. He showed his concern for the development of his city and the betterment of the living conditions of its citizens.

In 1840, the royal government refused to let Marseille have a railway station as a punishment for the city not having supported the Revolution which had brought King Louis-Philippe to power. Bishop de Mazenod took the defense of his city in hand and wrote a letter to the king requesting the much-needed railway station:

"*How pleased I would be if my observations would cause the king to change a plan which would be so damaging to our city! Nobody would have any doubts as to what was the source of such a benefit and it would be the bishop in his solicitude for all the members of his flock, who would have procured it for his people. Everybody would benefit thereby*" (Diary, April 21, 1842).

In 1847, he felt duty-bound to be present for the inauguration of the new water works which would enable the city to have a running water supply throughout the year and he made a public speech on that occasion:

"This inauguration is one of the most beautiful days in the history of Marseille. This magnificent work, fruit of the foresight and solicitude of its elected representatives, is one which will greatly improve the living conditions of the people of Marseille, a matter which is very close to our heart" (Diary of 1847).

In 1848, the French Republic organized general elections and, for the first time, all French citizens were invited to vote. While most of the bishops held reservations on the question, Bishop de Mazenod addressed a letter to all the people of his diocese inviting them to vote, *"for the welfare of all."* He even went further:

"On the Sunday on which the general elections are being held, the faithful will make every effort to reconcile their obligation to hear Mass with that of casting their vote. However, those who find it impossible to do so are dispensed from the obligation of hearing Mass because of the great importance of their duty to vote" (Lenten Pastoral, 1848).

The day fixed for the election was not just an ordinary Sunday, it was Easter Day!

On November 25, 1850, he inaugurated a new quarantine hospital on the island of Frioul in the bay of Marseille, and in doing so he took advantage of the occasion to remind the hospital staff of the mission which was theirs:

"In this place, the sick person must not be treated as a vile creature made only of matter, but as a being made in the image and likeness of the Creator. It is only in this way that true charity can be practiced" (Diary of 1850).

Bishop de Mazenod also took a deep interest in the rural population and in the immigrants who came to seek their fortune in Marseille. He showed concern for their accommodation which was often unhealthy. He established a movement to provide accommodation for working class people and laid the first stone of a model house. He blessed a housing estate which was to provide decent living conditions for workers in the naval yards. On that occasion he made a speech proclaiming the true human dignity of the worker and by so doing he incurred the displeasure of the prefect who denounced him to the Ministry of the Interior as a dangerous agitator. The aged prelate, now in his 76th year, had lost none of the energy of the young missionary who 45 years earlier had proclaimed in the Church the Madeleine: *"the eminent dignity of the poor of Jesus Christ."*

A Meditation in the Company
of St. Eugene

St. Eugene,
you never despaired of this world for the
simple reason that God declared his love for it.

I seem to hear you say:
"Brothers and sisters, come,
Be joyful in this world which God loves,
the great city of human beings
where God has pitched his tent
    and raised his Cross.
Go out to this world of violence
and tell it that peace has a right
    of residence in it!
Go out to this world with its many faces
and tell it that a welcoming hand has
    the right of residence!
Go out to this world of great loneliness
and tell it that love has the right
    of residence in it.

May all your lives be open
    to welcoming others.
May all your lives be peace for others.
In all your lives may your hearts
    be open to others.
May all your lives be an expression
    of trust in others."

"If I speak in human and angelic tongues but do not have charity, I am a resounding gong or a clashing cymbal.... If I have all faith so as to move mountains but do not have love, I am nothing. If I give away everything I own, and if I hand my body over so that I may boast but do not have charity, I gain nothing" (1 Cor 13:1–3).

Reflection Questions

How do I show love to those who are important to me? In what ways do I give of my talents to help those in need? Is there something that I need to let go of before I can love myself? What can I do today to bring God's love into someone's life?

10
Faithful When
the Storm Strikes

Focus Point

////////////

Life isn't easy for anyone. It takes courage and prayer to keep going amid the storms of life. Even though others may leave us, God will never abandon us.

////////////

"*I needed a special grace not to quarrel openly with the Archbishop for letting himself be influenced to such an extent by the passions of men who for a long time have impeded and persecuted us. This was the greatest sacrifice of self-love which I have made for a very long time. His Excellency put all the blame on me.*

"*But the missions, the Congregation, all those who are still awaiting salvation through our ministry! That nailed me to the cross which my nature could scarcely bear*" (Letter to Fr. Tempier, October 19, 1817).

////////////

A quick glance at the life of Eugene de Mazenod might give the impression that, after his return to God in 1807, everything was easy for him. In fact, at every stage of his life he had to face the storms which could have wiped out all that he had begun and, often too, threatened what he had achieved.

Starting in 1816, the storms began to blow, when he and the first missionaries took up residence in the former Carmelite convent in Aix. The success of his work was there for all to see and those who had been alienated from the Church flocked back to hear about Jesus Christ. However, that proved not to be to everyone's liking and he had to face up to the onslaught of the parish priests of Aix who accused him of emptying their churches. Some bishops even went so far as to declare that the vows taken in the Congregation were null and the Archbishop of Aix treated Eugene as "a hypocrite, a miserable being and a whitened sepulchre!" Eugene was tempted to react violently since he had never before been insulted in such a way. Had he not, however, decided to follow Christ? It was natural, therefore, that God should take him seriously and *"lead him along the path taken by the divine Master:*

"My God, what further graces would I have owed you if I had been accused of being possessed by the devil? Such a further mark of similarity to my Master would have given me a still greater hope

of recompense!" (Letter to Fr. Courtès, October 23–25, 1823).

In spite of the injury and hurt to his pride, he did not lose courage:

"*I am not downcast.... Our Society is strongly assailed by the tempest but let us not lose courage.... It is not difficult to perceive in all this a kind of aversion for the evangelical counsels and that makes me hope that He who first made them honorable will take in hand the defense of his work*" (Letter to Fr. Courtès, October 23–25, 1823).

He had to keep his mind at rest and carry on courageously; these were the conclusions he reached in the crisis.

Scarcely had that storm abated than another blew up in 1823. This time the trouble came from within his religious family. One of his companions in founding the Congregation, a man in whom he had placed all his trust, abandoned his vows and left the group. He was the first to do so but, alas, not the last. Eugene's fatherly heart was deeply wounded because he saw the event as a betrayal. It was a betrayal of the family, a betrayal of Christ, a betrayal of the poor.

"*It is indeed a monstrous infamy which I can hardly believe to be possible.... I can think of no greater outrage to the divinity, to the sacredness of the oath and to religion of which it makes a mockery*" (Letter to Fr. Courtès, October 9, 1823).

But he recovered his calm once again: it was an intuition coming from God which had started the Congregation. It had been the sight of the miseries in the Church, it was his desire to speak of Christ which had launched him on this venture. Therefore things were no longer in his power but in the hands of God. More than ever his attitude was *"to ask God to keep him as the apple of his eye."*

Another storm was on the way. This time the blow came from civil society with the Revolution of 1830. The new regime, at least at the beginning, was very anti-clerical. Mission crosses were pulled down, bishops' houses were sacked, parish priests were attacked, and processions were forbidden. Oblate works were shaken to their roots. Catastrophe closed the house in Nimes and interrupted parish missions. Discretion became the order of the day and the young men in formation had to be protected. Having attended to immediate needs, Eugene, once again, left the rest to divine Providence.

"In the name of God, let none of this turmoil upset or hinder a regular life. These circumstances require us to be as careful as necessary, but our devotion must not in any way be diminished" (Letter to Fr. Tempier, August 13, 1830).

A final tornado struck Eugene de Mazenod in 1832. The Pope, at the height of his quarrel with King Louis-Philippe, decided to show his independence by appointing a bishop in France without the king's consent. Eugene de Mazenod was the candidate chosen and he accepted *"for the good of the Church and because it is the desire of the Pope.*" The civil authority felt hurt and proceeded to react. It brought a case against the new bishop and deprived Eugene of his French citizenship. Eugene decided to defend himself against the injustice and illegality of the accusations.

Meanwhile, relations between the king and the Pope improved. The case of Eugene de Mazenod, the bishop against the royal dignity, became a nuisance item in Vatican diplomacy. It was pointed out to him that he should not pursue his defense "so as not to displease the Holy Father." Realizing that he had been "dropped" by the Pope whom he had served, Eugene obeyed:

"So as not to cause the least suffering to the Holy Father, I have ordered my lawyer to drop the case.... The Pope was displeased with me! He shall never be so again. My submission to his will is complete" (Letter to Bishop Frezza, November 28, 1834).

Nevertheless, he suffered terribly. He could never have believed that the Pope could do him such an injustice. He obeyed the successor of Peter but he made it clear that the decision was iniquitous and he felt totally disillusioned:

"I accept and I abandon myself to divine Providence. I wish I could add, 'and to the benevolence of the Holy Father,' but henceforth I hope for little from that quarter.... I know that, if I am exiled from my country, I should not count on the favor of the Holy Father nor on his good graces; my reward must come from God" (Letter to Bishop Frezza, November 28, 1834).

From this final storm as from all the others there is one conclusion which he was to draw:

"God has led me by the hand; and has had me accomplish so many things for his glory! Better for me those others should be unjust and ungrateful. In this way God will be my only reward, just as God is my only strength and my only hope" (Letter to Bishop Frezza, April 27, 1835).

A Meditation in the Company of St. Eugene

St. Eugene,
from time to time come back to me
    and say once again,
whenever the tempest rocks the boat
    of my life violently,
may the Lord always be on board.
Come back once again and say to me,
when the winds blow strong and seem
    to sink all that I have planned,
that the Lord be the only overseer
    of my work.

Come to me again and say,
when I am disillusioned by the collapse
    of my closest friendships,
that the Lord is the only faithful friend.

"I raise my eyes toward the mountains.
From where will my help come?

My help comes from the Lord
the maker of heaven and earth.

The Lord will guard you from all evil,
will always guard your life.
The Lord will guard your coming
  and going
both now and forever"
(Ps 121).

Reflection Questions

What has helped me weather the storms of
my life? What prayers do I pray during difficult times? If I am still angry over a situation,
can I ask God for the grace to let go of my
resentment?

11
Faithful during Times of Darkness

Focus Point

////////////

Sometimes doubts or sadness feel overwhelming and prayers do not bring comfort. Like Jesus in the Garden of Gethsemane, we cry out to God who seems to have abandoned us. Like Jesus, our faithfulness in the darkness will bring a new hope.

////////////

"When will my anguish come to an end? For several months now there has not been a day that has not brought bitterness. Past, present and future weigh upon my heart. I do not see how I can continue to exist. Ah, if only the good God had wished me to die, what a lot of displeasure I would have been spared! But may his holy will be done! I say that in perfect trust, in spite of all the rebellious thoughts arising from my nature whose legitimate feelings are frustrated" (Letter to Fr. Jeancard, September 26, 1829).

//////////////

*T*he period was the late 1820s. The Founder had already felt deeply hurt by the mis-understandings and the attacks from outside but now the trouble came from what he held most dear: his religious family. Having already had some of his sons depart the religious life, he now had to face up to a new trial: the death of four of the youngest Oblates, one of whom he saw as his spiritual son: Fr. Suzanne:

"*My dearly-beloved son, who can console me at your loss! Not even the thought of the eternal happiness you enjoy can bring me consolation! … Are you not always present in my thoughts?*" (Footnote in the Letter to Fr. Courtès, February 19, 1829).

This death was a very severe blow to him. Both his physical and psychological health were affected. He had no more zest for anything. He did not want to see anybody. Unceasingly the memory of "his deceased children" occupied his mind and pervaded his thoughts. He felt useless and even went so far as to question the value of all he had done since his ordination.

"*I put up with the burden but the sense of boredom and distaste is too much. I have reached the point where I need all my reasoning powers and a little of God's help in order not to declare 'that is enough' and say goodbye to the whole company*" (Letter to Fr. Courtès, May 28, 1824).

In prayer and in the celebration of the Eucharist, he experienced total spiritual dryness. All that he had done during the fifteen years of his ministry seemed of little value. He *"sighed because it seemed to him that he had not justified his existence."* Was it possible that he had made a mistake and that he would have been better off to have sought refuge in a monastery where he could bury himself in silence and prayer? Everything seemed to be crumbling to pieces around him and he even began to have doubts about his companions in the religious life:

"I have labored at training a few children, most of whom are incapable of conceiving the great ideals which would raise them above their milieu.... Wretched are these times and detestable is the influence of this age on minds! I ask God to take me out of this world if I am not to do anything more" (Letter to Fr. Tempier, August 1, 1830).

On the advice of his closest collaborators, Eugene went to the mountains of Switzerland to rest. Even there he did not find the peace he longed for. He was now in the darkest night of the soul, a state of spiritual distress which he had never before experienced and which became increasingly unbearable.

He had now reached the evening of Holy Thursday in the Garden of Gethsemane. When he had undertaken to follow the Son of God on the path of obedience to the will of his Father, he never thought it would take him so far in the imitation of Jesus Christ. He experienced in the very depths of his being the sentiments of the

Lord even to the point of only being able to pro-
nounce the very words of Jesus in the Garden
of Olives:

*"As long as these blows were falling upon me from
outside, I did not pay much attention to them. Now,
however, that Satan has decided to rain his arrows at
me from within the family, I feel afflicted to the point of
saying together with the Savior: 'My soul is sorrowful
even unto death'"* (Letter to Fr. Mye, October 31, 1832).

Passing through this absolute darkness, the
feelings of distaste and wanting to abandon
everything led him to realize that he could not
depend on any human consolation, and made
him totally free in the Spirit. After several months
of crisis, he at last became, like Christ his Lord,
totally open to the action of the Spirit:

*"Henceforth it is the Spirit who must be the abso-
lute Master of my soul, the only mover of my thoughts,
desires, affections and of my whole will"* (Retreat Notes,
May 1837).

The dark night of Christ had become his.
Until now he had not gone so far in experiencing
the accomplishment of the will of the Father. He
had to descend to the very depths of this night to
cry out in perfect freedom and to be able to say:

*"I feel that I am now dealing with my Father....
May his will be done"* (Letter to Fr. Tempier, October
10, 1832).

From that point onwards, Eugene became a
man who was really free to follow the will of

God because he was in close communion with what God expected of him. In all his missionary letters he would refer to this personal experience. Having experienced the dark night of the soul, that unique moment when all was silence, when no human support was possible, when the only motive for saying "yes" was absolute confidence which had no intellectual or sentimental justification, he now knew what he was talking about when he recommended that his missionaries be totally abandoned to the will of God.

It was the outcome of a long and tough struggle, of a shedding of his will by which he placed himself totally in God's hands, because God was God and that was sufficient for him.

Accepting God's will after the dark night of the soul still meant much suffering for Eugene, because, however much he may have been attuned to the ways of Providence, he *"was not less sad for the rest of his life when he lost those who were dear to him."* He could never really understand why God should require that he suffer such separations.

His acceptance did not amount to resignation. It was simply a trusting confidence, so much so that, even in the midst of the darkest depths of God's silence, he was capable of exclaiming:

"You, my God, are my only hope and I know from experience that you will never let me down" (Retreat Notes, October 7–14, 1832).

He experienced God in the depth of his silence. It took a painful transformation of his conscience and of his awareness of the world to make him enter the mystery of his belonging to God. He devoted all his resources, his psychological and physical faculties and his social existence to one purpose only: to succeed in encountering Christ. Such an encounter was possible only through an act of absolute love; that was love itself, loving above all else, to the point where the one loved revealed himself and took the lover out of and beyond himself.

He was overwhelmed by the *"indispensable need to imitate Jesus Christ"*:

"Let us bow down, listen respectfully, admire in silence. Let us swear to be faithful and to become worthy of this great vocation" (Retreat Notes, October 1831).

God listened to his request and took it seriously.

A Meditation in the Company of St. Eugene

St. Eugene,

how often has it happened that I too have been completely disturbed by God's silence! When I experience distaste for prayer, when the misfortunes of life besiege me, in the presence of old age, sickness or mourning, it often happens that I no longer understand and I have the impression that God is silent.

It is then that I need you to help me hear the voice of God who seems to be silent and to read the presence of the Holy One when God seems to be absent.

You have felt the dizziness of the absolute. Teach me not to be afraid of it.

You have experienced what it means to hope against all hope. Teach me to follow this path which is the road to life.

I shall then be able to be free as you were. I shall then be able to be open to the Spirit. I shall then be able to let the Son say in me: "Father, glorify your Name."

"There was then a great wind which rent the mountains and broke the rocks, but God was not in the wind.

After the wind there was an earthquake, but God was not in the earthquake.

After the earthquake there was a great fire, but God was not in the fire.

Then, in the silence, there was a tiny whispering sound of a light breeze.

When he heard this, he came out and stood at the entrance of the cave. And the voice of God came to him" (1 Kgs 19:11–13).

Reflection Questions

What has been my experience of "God's silence?" Can I pray for myself, or ask others to pray for me? How have I been able to cope with the death of a loved one? At this moment, I will offer a prayer for someone who is struggling with a difficult time in their life.

12
Faithful
in Everyday Matters

Focus Point

////////////

Daily matters can drain a person of enthusiasm, especially when there is an imbalance between work, prayer and leisure. As the years bring changes, we must re-evaluate how to nourish our daily life.

////////////

"I find things so worrisome that I have reached the point of no longer having the inner peace which should be my consolation and my happiness. If that is how things are, then what good can I do to others? I merely work like a machine in matters that concern me personally.... It seems I only love God in fits and starts. I pray badly, meditate badly, prepare badly for Holy Mass, I say it badly" (Retreat Notes, May 1818).

////////////

*P*erhaps it is easier to be faithful, when the tempest threatens to sink the boat. Perhaps it is easier to hold on in the darkness of the night, when the tempest is so strong that there is nothing else to which to hold on to except God. There is, however, another risk to fidelity, a risk which is much more subtle and dangerous: the risk brought about by the ordinariness of every-day life. It is a sort of slow wearing away which dampens enthusiasm, and can remain unno-ticed. It is like a fine powder which gradually covers everything and, without our noticing it, weighs upon our mind in a thousand little ways and erodes love from our heart.

During his long life, Eugene de Mazenod had to run that risk also. Three years after his ordination, his activities were crowding in upon him and his impassioned love for human beings tended to make him overlook the real reason for which he had developed that love: his headlong love of God and for God. When he found the time to take stock of the situation, he realized that his accounts needed balancing, because "by working too much for others, he has been too forgetful of himself and he has almost neglected his spiritual life":

"It is good to be always available to serve one's neighbor, but this service has become a real slavery. If complacency is taken too far it becomes weakness. I shall have to work out a plan of action for myself" (Retreat Notes, December 1814).

In his intense love for human beings, for whose dignity and development he strove, he ran the risk of emptying all that he did of its meaning by letting himself be dragged into activism. He had to struggle to find time for prayer, for the re-evaluation of his days in the light of the Gospel.

"*As for this neighbor whom I am supposed to love, I often come away from him feeling useless for anything. It should not be that way. The proof of that is in the fact that, when I spend a day on my own, things are better afterwards*" (Retreat Notes, December 1814).

Another form of routine is spiritual burnout. Everyone has experienced in life the better moments when God seems to be very near. Then daily events take over and these moments become increasingly distant memories which gradually cease to nourish our lives. Eugene de Mazenod was not to escape this either:

"*I have experienced spiritual weariness, a sort of torpor.... How have I been doing my times of adoration? I have not gained any enlightenment from them, nor any tender feelings, nor any consolation*" (Retreat Notes, December 1814).

He recovered, he became once again enthusiastic about rediscovering how sweet it is to let God take over his prayer life and the extent to which that gave meaning to his whole existence. Once again, however, the humdrum of life began to take over and shortly afterwards he repeated the same statement:

"*I pray badly, I meditate badly, I prepare badly for the celebration of Holy Mass, I say it badly, I make my thanksgiving badly. In everything I have a feeling of aversion to recollecting myself ...*" (Retreat Notes, May 1818).

To conquer this spiritual weariness, he once again immersed himself endlessly in marvelling at the infinite love of God. He was not afraid to review his infidelities, his lukewarmness, his lack of courage in the past. In fact, the more he saw himself as he really was, the more astonished he was that God still loved him. Each of his periods of "spiritual lukewarmness" caused him to rediscover the ever new presence of Christ in his life:

"*O Lord, shine upon me a beam of your light so that I can know myself as I really am in your eyes. O my God, the more I remember my sins, the more I am aware of your mercy, because you are my God!*" (Retreat Notes, May 1824).

Another source of wear and tear was that caused by age. As the years went by, his physical and spiritual forces became less. A need for peace and quiet began to replace the daring of earlier years. Zeal became muted and mediocrity, insidiously, began to take over:

"*At the beginning of my ministry, I took off at a gallop, and the speed at which I travelled most likely prevented me from seeing the obstacles along the way.*

I hardly gave them a thought, either because of my own rashness or because there were so many other things to think about. I had little fear of them. Now, that I move with short steps, things are quite different. One by one I count the stumbling blocks, the branches which overhang my path, the thorns which pierce me to the bone, the cold which freezes me, the heat which stifles me, the illnesses which weaken me, the infirmities which overwhelm me" (Diary, August 1, 1837).

It was in 1837 that Eugene wrote these lines, at the time when, in order to serve the Church, he had accepted one of the heaviest burdens in the Church, the episcopacy of Marseille, the second largest city in France. It was at that point that he set out with renewed enthusiasm on the path of the mission *"because* (a bishop) *must love to the end, even to the extent of giving his life for the people who have been entrusted to his care."*

He did not consider his fitness for the office entrusted to him to be as important as his availability to fulfill the will of God:

"I must therefore move forward, that is the necessity imposed on me by God. Have courage then, and rely upon his grace" (Retreat Notes, May 1837).

To succeed in doing so:

"It is sufficient for me to acknowledge that, through his grace, I am different today to what I was once upon a time. Now my reply to this new call of the Master shall be: 'Here I am.' But, O Lord, help me, come yourself to my help" (Retreat Notes, May 1837).

Finally, the experience of everyday life tended to lead him into another sort of weariness: that caused by human beings themselves.

Life did not spare Eugene de Mazenod this type of weariness either. His heart was made to love but all too often his love was not reciprocated and he met with great disappointment. Not only did it happen that people failed to acknowledge his kindness but things went even further than that. In 1838, a former employee at the bishop's house, whom he had helped in a special way, started a particularly infamous campaign against him. He was severely tempted to renounce his faith in human beings and to retire to his "ivory tower":

"Sometimes when I am tempted to do good to human beings out of compassion for them and to please them or make them happy, then the memory of ungrateful persons prevents me from giving anything. I feel that my heart is becoming hardened towards the miseries of humanity" (Diary, April 7, 1838).

Once again Eugene's following of Christ was to help him get out of the routine where human meanness threatened to drag him down. Christ had only one attitude: he loved without expecting anything in return. He loved because he is love. If Eugene de Mazenod was to continue imitating Christ, he would have to continue to love human beings, "love them always, love them in spite of everything."

Thus he was able to reach the evening of his life still loving human beings just as he had loved them in the enthusiasm of his youth and even begging their pardon for not having loved them enough:

"*I ask pardon of all those who believe I have hurt them, of those whom I have hurt and even made unhappy, and I proclaim that it has been in spite of myself and without any intention of doing so that I have displeased them*" (Last Will and Testament, August 1, 1854).

A Meditation in the Company of St. Eugene

St. Eugene,

on the day of your Canonization, Pope John Paul II said that you were a man of Advent, a man of the Coming. Your life was a waiting and a welcoming for the Son of Man who came into this world, as you waited for your sons who came to meet you.

By following your example may I become a man, or a woman, of Advent. I shall then be able to get away from my spiritual routine and be ready every day to welcome anyone who knocks on my door.

By following your example may I become a man, or a woman, of Advent. I shall then welcome each day as a further challenge in the adventure of life.

By following your example, may I become a man, or a woman, of Advent. I shall then be able to overcome my disappointments and welcome all who come to me, to love them always, to love them in spite of everything.

"Be diligent in the pursuit of justice, piety, faith, charity, constancy, and gentleness. Fight the good fight of faith, win for yourself the eternal life to which you have been called and in view of which you made your profession of faith in the presence of many witnesses. I beg you before God, who gives life to all things, and before Christ Jesus, who, under Pontius Pilate, gave such beautiful witness, keep the commandments without stain or reproach until the appearance of our Lord Jesus Christ" (1 Tim 6:11–14).

Reflection Questions

When life is busy do I abandon enriching my spiritual life? How do I balance work, prayer and leisure? What changes have I noticed as I get older? Can I love without expecting anything in return?

13

Strengthened by the Eucharist

Focus Point

//////////////

The Eucharist gives a person strength to overcome his or her sinful actions; it is not a reward for one who is perfect. By the Eucharist we are transformed by God and united to one another.

//////////////

"Everything leads up to the Eucharist. That is where God finds his glory and man his salvation. All the Sacraments, all God's gifts, all works of true piety, are pointed in this direction. It is there we find the summit of our sanctification, the crowning of our glorification and the perfection of God's glory among humanity" (Christmas Pastoral, 1859).

//////////////

E ugene de Mazenod lived at a time when frequent Communion was practically unheard of. He reacted against this situation because he was very conscious of his own sinfulness and his inability to escape from it without God's help. The Eucharist is not "*a recompense provided for holy people*" but "*salvation offered to sinners.*"

"*Perfection depends on frequenting the Sacraments and frequenting the Sacraments does not depend on perfection.... Each Communion is a preparation for the one to follow and it is only possible to learn to love Christ worthily by receiving this Sacrament of his love*" (Letter to Mrs. de Boisgelin, December 4, 1808).

The human being's destiny is to share in the divine life and to be united with God as from today, in our everyday existence because this world has been willed by God and his Son has made it his dwelling place.

"*The Eucharist is the means he has given us that we may live in his Spirit*" (Letter to Mrs. de Boisgelin, December 4, 1808).

His Good Friday experience caused Eugene to discover his sinfulness and also to discover his destiny of union with God. The Eucharist became for him the place where the creature could finally reach beyond his or her sin and become what he or she was destined to be:

"*Let us receive the Eucharist frequently; that is the only way to become saints!*" (Letter to Mrs. de Boisgelin, September 19, 1811).

The weaker we feel, the more we should approach the "*only source of our sanctification*":

"*How blind we are, to have there with us the well-spring of all consolation and to persist in our refusal to approach it and draw water. 'Come to me,' the Spouse continually exclaims. 'Come to me all you who suffer life's woes and who are afflicted, and I will give you rest.' ... I am the bread of life. I am the strength of the weak. I am the support of all*" (Letter to his grandmother Joannis, December 3, 1810).

The Eucharist, for Eugene de Mazenod, was also the means to accomplish his mission of converting and sanctifying other human beings. As a preacher of the Word and an artisan of charity, he was convinced that his mission could only be effective through the Eucharist:

"*I shall convert more souls by my devotion to the Eucharist than by all the preaching I am able to do. Nothing gives more glory to God or is more effective for the salvation of souls than the Mass*" (Retreat Notes, December 1812).

Eugene de Mazenod, as bishop, devoted his last teaching to the Eucharist which he presented as the summit of the whole Christian life:

"*All the Sacraments of the Church, all the supernatural gifts of God, all works of true piety are focused on the Eucharist, which is the cause and the consummation of our sanctification, the crowning of our glory, the perfection of the glory of God among human beings*" (Lenten Pastoral, 1859).

It is in this Sacrament that the work of our divinization, begun in Baptism, is accomplished. For that reason, nobody should be prevented from sharing the Lord's Body, whether it is the dying or the worst of sinners. Once, when he had given Communion to a person condemned to death, he wrote:

"*This man who has received the Body of Christ is worthy of admiration, a privileged being for whom the Lord has done great things, a predestined soul who would probably be in heaven in a few days*" (Diary, July 16, 1837).

For Eugene de Mazenod, the Eucharist was a means of sanctification and it was also the special place for an intimate meeting, his heart-to-heart talks with the Lord.

On a number of occasions he had intense mystical experiences when celebrating the Eucharist or receiving Communion.

On Christmas Day, 1811, when celebrating his first Mass he experienced "*transports of love and gratitude.*"

In 1825, when he undertook the necessary steps to have the Congregation recognized by the Pope, it was the Eucharist which gave him strength and courage at a time when there seemed to be little hope of success:

"*It was at the time of Communion that our divine Savior gave me the greatest proof of his love. It was by abandoning myself to feeling his divine presence and the immensity of his mercy that I was inspired in those moments*" (Letter to Fr. Tempier, February 16, 1826).

When he was anxiously awaiting the decision of the cardinals who were examining the Constitutions of the Oblates of Mary Immaculate, in February, 1826, it was the Eucharist which enabled him to abandon himself trustingly to God's will:

"*During the time of their meeting ... I stayed in the church of Santa Maria in Campitelli and I had plenty of time to hear nine Masses. I assure you, however, that since I had gone in there with the intention of waiting, I was not bored in the slightest. On the contrary, I felt quite at ease in that beautiful church, doing what one would wish to be doing always*" (Letter to Fr. Tempier, February 16, 1826).

In August, 1830, at the time when he was in the depths of the dark night of the soul, the Eucharist remained the special place where he met with the Lord:

"*This morning, before receiving Communion, I dared to speak to my good Master with the same abandon as I would have done if I had the happiness of living while he was on this earth, and I was in the same predicament as I am today.... I made known our needs, I asked for light and assistance, and then I abandoned myself entirely to the Lord, not wishing for anything other than God's holy will.... I then received Communion in that frame of mind. At that moment I received an abundance of interior consolation. There were no painful thoughts! On the contrary, I felt good,*

I was happy, I wanted to feel and I really did feel grateful" (Letter to Fr. Tempier, August 23, 1830).

The Eucharist became the *"delightful meeting place,"* the *"community center where we came together each day"*:

"You know that you are always present in my thoughts, in the morning during the Holy Sacrifice and in the evening during adoration before the tabernacle. This meeting place is the only means of overcoming distances, being at the same time in the presence of the Lord, meeting, as it were, side-by-side. We cannot see one another but we feel our presence, we can hear one another, we mingle in the same place" (Letter to Fr. de L'Hermite, January 10, 1852).

Eugene de Mazenod invites us to abide in the Eucharist as the one place which brings together our persons, our communities, our prayers and our activities. That is where our scattered forces come together. That is where we gain fresh courage. That is where we let ourselves be totally transformed, where we are made divine by our only Lord and Savior.

"To unite yourself with Christ in Communion is to come back to life. What a perfect renewal is brought about in you! Then you taste peace, a peace which surpasses sentiment, which stimulates recollection in your prayer and increases the ardor of your charity" (Lenten Pastoral, 1859).

A Meditation in the Company
of St. Eugene

St. Eugene,

one day a bishop said of you that you had a heart as big as that of St. Paul, the Apostle who wrote: "It is no longer I who live; but Christ lives in me!"

"It is no longer I who live; but Christ lives in me!"

How am I to make place for Christ, to have him live totally in me, if the Eucharist is not the heart and center of my life?

"It is no longer I who live; but Christ lives in me!"

How is it possible to have a heart-to-heart intimacy with the Lord if I do not take time to pause, to adore the Holy One in the Eucharistic presence?

"It is no longer I who live; it is Christ who lives in me!"

How can I become, as Christ was, totally devoted to others if I do not receive the bread which was broken, the wine spilled in abundance for the salvation of the world?

"*The Eucharist is, of course, food for my soul and the treasure of my heart. It is there I find my support, my consolation, my friend, the source of all graces and all delights*" (Note written on the Register in the monastery of the Sacramentines of Marseille, July 25, 1847).

"When they were at table, Christ took bread, said the blessing, broke it and gave it to them.

With that their eyes were opened and they recognized him, but he vanished from their sight.
Then they said to each other, 'Were not our
hearts burning within us while he spoke to us
on the way and opened the scriptures to us?'

"So they set out at once and returned to
Jerusalem where they found gathered together
the eleven with their companions. Then the two
recounted what had taken place on the way and
how they had recognized the Lord in the break-
ing of bread" (Lk 24:30–35).

Reflection Questions

Do I receive the Eucharist to strengthen me
with God's spirit? Am I able to speak openly
to God? Eugene took time during Adoration to
also be present to those he held dear. Do I do
the same?

14
Journeying Together as Companions

Focus Point

////////////

To do God's will is not a solitary task for me. Companions will join me on this journey. Some will be of my choosing and others will not; both deserve my respect.

////////////

"*I do not know how my heart suffices to hold the affection it sustains for all of you. There is no other creature on earth on whom God has bestowed the favor of loving so tenderly, so strongly, such a great number of persons. This is not merely a question of charity but of a maternal affection which I have for each one of you without prejudice for the others. None of you can be loved more than I love you. I love each one of you to the full, as though he was the only one loved, and I experience this very demanding love for every one. It is just wonderful!*" (Letter to Fr. Mouchette, April 24, 1855).

////////////

*E*ugene de Mazenod intended to join the diocesan clergy and in the first years of his ministry he worked alone, among the young people, the prisoners or the people at home. He discovered, however, that he was beginning to lose any "spirit of the interior life" because of the cares of his mission:

"*I no longer act as anything other than a machine in matters which concern me personally. It seems to me that I am no longer able to think when it comes to things which concern my own welfare. If that is true, what good can I be to others?*" (Retreat Notes, May 1818).

What had to be done in order to devote himself totally to others while at the same time remaining fully united with Christ? How could he do all that he had to do without being overtaken by activism instead of being concerned solely for the glory of God? He found the answer to this question in the Gospel:

"*What did Our Lord Jesus Christ do? He chose a number of apostles and disciples whom he himself trained in piety, and he filled them with his spirit. These men he sent forth, once they had been schooled in his teaching, to conquer the world ...*" (Oblate Rule of 1818).

The mission was no longer a personal matter. Based on the model of the Twelve Apostles, as instituted by the Savior, the community was to become the sign and the bearer of the mission:

"We wish to choose men who will have the strength and the courage to walk in the footsteps of the Apostles" (Letter to Fr. Tempier, October 9, 1815).

In the request which he addressed to the Vicars General of Aix-en-Provence on January 25, 1816, Eugene emphasized the idea that he wished to found a community with a view to the mission:

"The missionaries ask you to authorize them to live in community....

"Their preference is to form a regular community of Missionaries in order to serve the diocese and, at the same time, work for their own sanctification....

"It is in community that they wish to acquire the virtues and the knowledge worthy of a good missionary ..." (Letter to the Capitular Vicars General, Oblate Writings, Vol. 13, No. 2).

He was aware that his companions, like himself, had their limitations. Like him, they were *"almost good for nothing."* He knew very well that *"the little good that they do, they do it because the good God grabs them by the shoulders and pushes them.* They were, however, the brothers whom God had given him to love. What was important was that they should form a community where love would reign. In that way they would be a sign of that great family which God wanted to bring together by gathering his scattered children.

Because the choice came from God *"we must love one another as brothers. This mutual affection will make us happy, holy and strong to do good work."*

Eugene de Mazenod considered that it would be an illusion to think that he could bring the Gospel to the world, if he did not first of all have a deep love for all the brothers whom God had given him in his religious family:

"Often I have told the good Lord that, since he has given me a mother's heart and sons who merit my love under so many titles, God must allow me to love them immeasurably. This I do in good conscience. It seems to me that the more I love beings such as they are, the more and the better I love God" (Letter to Fr. Mouchette, March 22, 1857).

Such a love could only come from God and therefore, in the eyes of men it expressed that God is love. A community, where this love coming from God was supreme, was by its very existence, missionary. Love within and zeal abroad are but one and the same unique reality, and the last words of St. Eugene were:

"Among yourselves practice charity, charity, charity, and abroad, zeal for the salvation of souls."

It was because he loved the brothers whom God had entrusted to him that he could reprimand them energetically, and his angry outbursts were famous. It was because he felt a special tenderness for each one that he could afford to do so. He wanted them to grow in maturity and not to waste any of the talents they possessed. It was by no means a rare occurrence that, having severely chastised one of his brothers, he would go on his knees before him to ask his pardon.

In prayer he kept in touch with all his brothers, he welcomed their visits, their letters. He suffered as a result of their shortcomings in fraternal charity or their lukewarmness in the mission. He was conscious of his indebtedness to them and he unceasingly thanked God who had given him companions such as these:

"I belong above all and principally to this family for whom the Lord has given me so much love and which is for me constantly and so justly an object of admiration....

"They all have incomparably more virtue than I, and I could well say that I am not worthy to untie the straps of their sandals. How happy I count myself to be one of their number! What thanks do I not owe to God for having given them to me. I will therefore always live in a spirit of the most intimate union with them" (Retreat Notes, May 1824).

He invited others to do likewise and to acknowledge in others the wonders worked by God:

"Always have a great deference and respect for one another. Be convinced that no one on this earth possesses every quality, be satisfied with those you have received, try to acquire more, but do not demand that your brother's share be numerically greater than your own. It is possible that he lacks some quality or virtue that you think you have. Rest assured that he, for his part, has some which you lack. Place all in common,

then, to everybody's advantage. You are all members of the same body. Let each one exercise his own talents and the whole body will then not lack anything" (Letter to Fr. Honorat, January 17, 1843).

On the day of our Baptism we were all given the mission to launch out into the deep, not as individuals but in the company of the brothers and sisters given to us by God. In receiving that mission we also received the Spirit who enables us to accept one another and be companions on the journey, each worthy of the respect and love of the others.

A Meditation in the Company of St. Eugene

St. Eugene,

you were decidedly not afraid to go counter to what the world of your day acclaimed.

When the world glories in its heroes who are self-made, often by crushing others, you whisper to me: "You cannot become what you should be except by allowing others to build you up, day by day."

When the world invites me to live in a cozy circle of friends or companions whom I have carefully selected, you whisper to me: "You can only grow to what you should be if you welcome all those whom God gives you as your life companions."

When the world seems to invite me to enclose myself in my own intellectual airspace, you whisper to me: "Open your doors and windows to all the richness, to all the qualities of the other person."

When the world appreciates each one only according to appearances, you whisper to me: "Find your worth in your brother or sister because, whatever personal virtues you may be lacking yourself, you can have the joy of seeing in the works and the holiness of others" (Letter to Fr. Honorat, January 17, 1843).

"Just as the body is one, although it has many parts, and all the parts of the body, though many, are one body, so it is with Christ. For in one Spirit we were all baptized into one body, whether Jews or Greeks, slaves or free persons, and we were all nourished by the same Spirit" (1 Cor 12:12–13).

Reflection Questions

Do I respect the talents of others, or am I sometimes envious of them? How do I acknowledge (compliment) the work of others? Do I work well with others or do I try to be the center of attention?

15
Journeying with Mary

Focus Point

//////////////

We usually think of Mary in her role as the human woman who gave birth to Jesus, our Savior. But Mary at the foot of the cross is a source of courage and comfort.

//////////////

"How I rejoice with the Holy Virgin Mary at the great things God has done in her. What a wonderful advocate we have with God! Let us be devoted to her. We profess to go to her Son through her and we hope for everything through her intercession" (Letter to his grandmother, October 18, 1808).

//////////////

Since he was the founder of a religious family placed under the auspices of Mary,

Eugene de Mazenod must evidently have given Mary a special position in his life. What was that position?

His first discovery was that of the Cross and his spirituality was decidedly Christological. In his contemplation of the Cross, however, he was led to look upon the Woman who was there beneath it, standing in silence. The Cross led him to Mary and he attributes a triple dimension to her presence.

Mary at the foot of the Cross was, for Eugene, the accomplishment of the "Yes" which she had uttered at the moment of the Annunciation. She became for him the model of his total gift of self to the Father. What had begun in her with the message of the archangel Gabriel and what had continued throughout Our Lord's public life had its crowning moment when she stood there silently, fully associating herself with Christ's offering of himself to his Father. The words uttered by the Son: "Father, may your will be done" became the words of the Mother. It was by being present at the offering of her Son and by associating herself with that offering that Mary entered fully into God's plan for her. She then became the model of the gift of self, following in the footsteps of Christ as he offered himself totally to his Father:

"*With Mary at the foot of the Cross, let us repeat unceasingly those words which so fittingly calm all our sorrows: 'May your will be done!'* " (Diary, January 3, 1859).

"*I am at present engaged in meditating on the offering of the Blessed Virgin at the foot of the Cross, about which, until now, I have had only a very vague idea*" (Letter to Fr. Courtès, January 29, 1829).

For Eugene, Mary at the foot of the Cross was also the person to whom Christ had given the prestigious title of "Woman," that is to say the "New Eve," the one who was to answer to God's merciful plan, the creature restored to the likeness of her Creator. She was Immaculate in her Conception. Eugene de Mazenod had been a defender of this title long before it had been proclaimed by the Church's teaching and it appeared to him as the consequence of the Cross. To say that Mary was the Immaculate Conception was to say that the act of saving the world was accomplished by Christ on the Cross and that, as a result, the whole world had been restored to its pristine dignity. Whatever our sin might be, and whatever might be our feeling of unworthiness, we could know that this restoration had taken place because God had already accomplished it for one of his creatures.

"*Oblate of Mary Immaculate, that is a passport for heaven! Let us be aware that it will be as glorious as it will be consoling for us to be consecrated to her in a special manner and to bear her name*" (Letter to Fr. Tempier, December 22, 1825).

Finally, Mary at the foot of the Cross was the Mother whom Jesus gave to all his brothers and sisters. She was the Mother of the new People of God, a people assembled by Christ, a people inhabited by the Spirit, a people impassioned for the glory of the Father.

For Eugene de Mazenod, Mary was, above all, the Mother given to us by Jesus:

"Remember that by adoring the Sacred Heart of Jesus you are drawing on God's love at its source, and that in paying homage to the heart of Mary, you are reminding her of the tenderness she showed for us on Calvary, when her Son gave us to her as her children" (Letter to Mrs. de Mazenod, end of April, 1809).

Eugene spoke to her as to a mother and he asked all his missionaries *to "have a tender devotion to her."* He lived in intimate union with her, telling her of his joys and sorrows, sharing with her his sufferings as well as his enthusiasm and his fears as a missionary.

He appealed to her as a mother to ask for vocations:

"Let us pray to the Father that he may send workers to cultivate the vineyard he has entrusted to us. It is our Mother who must obtain this grace for us so as to obtain the glory of her divine Son" (Letter to Fr. Tempier, April 13, 1826).

It is to her that he addressed his thanks for the results obtained in the different missions:

"As for me, I am quite convinced that we owe all this to the protection of our good Mother" (Letter to Fr. Guigues, September 25, 1844).

It was to her that he addressed his prayer as he approached the end of his life:

"Asking that my sins may be forgiven, I invoke the intercession of the Immaculate Virgin Mary, Mother of God, and I dare to remind her, in all humility, but filled with consolation, of my filial devotion throughout my life and the desire I have always had to make her known and loved" (Last Will and Testament, August 1, 1854).

Honoring Mary, and particularly in her Immaculate Conception, always meant referring in wonderment to the God who loves us so much that he died for us on the Cross:

"We must love and venerate the most Holy Virgin. In addressing your prayers to the Lord, recommend them to the powerful intercession of Mary. Let your trust always go straight to heaven and let it not dwell on a material image which does not of itself have any power whatever. That is what the pagans do in their error by glorifying their idols. It is not the image, not the statue which can hear your prayer. It is the Holy Virgin who listens to your petitions and will obtain help for you from God who is the only beginning and end of all power" (Christmas Pastoral, 1837).

The more he advanced in years, the more his prayer to Mary became tender and trusting. He could not contain his joy on learning that Pius IX was planning to proclaim the definition of the Immaculate Conception:

"Happy the day when God, through the Holy Spirit of his divine Son, inspired the heart of the Holy

Father to do this supreme honor to the Virgin Mary" (Letter to Pope Pius IX, 1851).

He received a personal invitation from the Holy Father to be present at the event on December 8, 1854, and his joy was like that of a child celebrating his mother's feast. At the same time he saw in the event the sign of the victory of the Cross over all the forces of death. As well as Mary, all of humanity had been snatched from the consequences of sin and was now glorified:

"I thought that the Church Suffering was enlightened at that moment by a divine illumination, that the sufferings of those souls was suspended. Purgatory was being emptied through the clemency of the divine judge who, on the occasion of his Mother's glorification, caused her whole family to share in the Church's joy. God pardoned all their debts and united them to the outbursts of joy in the choir of his angels and saints" (Rome Diary, December 8, 1854).

One of his last pastoral letters, written just one year before he died, was devoted to Mary and in it he asked the people of his diocese to attribute to Christ the graces obtained through Mary's intercession:

"The only reason we address our prayers to her with such confidence is so that she will intercede for us with her divine Son who is the only author of all grace" (Christmas Pastoral, 1859).

A Meditation in the Company
of St. Eugene

St. Eugene,

on May 21, 1861, the moment of your death had come. Your Oblates were there present. They intoned the ancient prayer of the Salve Regina, a hymn of trust in which human beings turn to their Mother in heaven. When they reached the threefold invocation to the clement, loving and sweet Virgin Mary, you finished your journey on this earth and, with Mary Immaculate, you hastened to meet your Lord.

Together with Saint Eugene, I greet you Mary, Mother of him who is all mercy. In you I greet the sign of a merciful God.

Together with Saint Eugene, I greet you Mary, Mother of him who is all sweetness. In you I greet the sign of a God who presses us to his heart.

Together with Saint Eugene, I greet you Mary, Mother of him who is all goodness. In you I greet the sign of a God who casts his loving look on each and every one.

Together with Saint Eugene, I greet you Mary, my Mother. I know that you are always at my side in this great journey of life.

I know that I can stretch out my hand to you as a child would to its mother, knowing you will give me your protection.

"Standing by the cross of Jesus stood his Mother.... When Jesus saw his mother and the disciple there whom he loved, he said to his mother, 'Woman, behold your son.' Then he said to the disciple, 'Behold your mother.' And from that hour the disciple took her into his home" (Jn 19:25–27).

Reflection Questions

What is my relationship with Mary? How is my "yes" to God similar to Mary's response to the will of God? How does Mary inspire my life? Which of the prayers to Mary give me comfort?

Also available in the
"15 Days of Prayer" series:

Saint Augustine *(Jaime García)*
0-7648-0655-6, paper

Saint Benedict *(André Gozier)*
978-1-56548-304-0, paper

Saint Bernadette of Lourdes *(François Vayne)*
978-1-56548-314-9, paper

Saint Bernard *(Emery Pierre-Yves)*
978-0764-805745, paper

Dietrich Bonhoeffer *(Matthiew Arnold)*
978-1-56548-311-8, paper

Saint Catherine of Siena *(Chantal van der
    Plancke and Andrè Knockaert)*
978-156548-310-1, paper

Pierre Teilhard de Chardin *(André Dupleix)*
978-0764-804908, paper

The Curé of Ars *(Pierre Blanc)*
978-0764-807138, paper

Saint Dominic *(Alain Quilici)*
978-0764-807169, paper

Saint Katharine Drexel *(Leo Luke Marcello)*
978-0764-809231, paper

Don Bosco *(Robert Schiele)*
978-0764-807121, paper

Charles de Foucauld *(Michael Lafon)*
978-0764-804892, paper

Saint Francis de Sales *(Claude Morel)*
978-0764-805752, paper

Saint John of the Cross *(Constant Tonnelier)*
978-0764-806544, paper

Saint Faustina Kowalska *(John J. Cleary)*
978-0764-807916, paper

Saint Louis de Montfort *(Veronica Pinardon)*
978-0764-807152, paper

Saint Martín de Porres: A Saint of the Americas *(Brian J. Pierce)*
978-0764-812163, paper

Meister Eckhart *(André Gozier)*
978-0764-806520, paper

Thomas Merton *(André Gozier)*
978-0764-804915, paper

Saint Elizabeth Ann Seton *(Betty Ann McNeil)*
978-0764-808418, paper

Johannes Tauler *(André Pinet)*
978-0764-806537, paper

Saint Teresa of Ávila *(Jean Abiven)*
978-0764-805738, paper

Saint Thérèse of Lisieux *(Constant Tonnelier)*
978-0764-804922, paper

Saint Thomas Aquinas *(André Pinet)*
978-0764-806568, paper